To the matriarchs,
to the political prisoners,
and to the martyrs
in five hundred years of resistance...
and counting.

The war against imperialism continues
and so do we

TRIBUNAL RISING

Eastwind Books
Berkeley, California

Eastwind Books First Edition
Printed in Abya Yala

ISBN: 9781961562110

Book Curator: Judith Talaugon
Book Editor: Angela Marino
Book Designer: Lulu Matute
Book Art Pages: Eleni Berg, Javier Mateos-Campos, and Lulu Matute

Contributing Authors: Dayani Albuquerque, Sarine Danielle Baronian, Delmi Belloso, Alexander Cole, Brandon Cruz, Muhammad Delgado, Keira Duong Lam, Theodore Dupont, B'eleje' Kan, Jonas Kramer, Angela Marino, Alexander Marsh, Javier Mateos-Campos, Lulu Matute, Ci Mingshu, Luis Alejandro Molina, Juna Park, Abby Román, Shaka Shakur, Judith Talaugon, and Jingyi Zhou

Contributing Editors: Muhammad Delgado, Anna Julian, Javier Mateos-Campos, Lulu Matute, and Leah Kiana Parvini

Art Exhibit Catalog
Archivist and Art Exhibit Coordinator: Nathaniel Moore
Assistant Curator: Joaquin Min Antonio
Speaker Event Coordinator/Interview: Seth Donnelly
Media: Javier Mateos-Campos and Priscilla Vasquez

Front Cover: Artwork on the front cover is designed by Lulu Matute and derived from the Sonoma County Free Press vol 6, No 4 1992. Artist of a portion of the original illustration is by Thomas Yeates whose art can be found at thomasyeates.com

TABLE OF CONTENTS

PART THREE | TRIBUNAL FRAMEWORKS CRITIQUE AND CREATE

ACKNOWLEDGEMENTS

To the tribunal organizers and judges, leaders of our future and past; to the archivists at The Freedom Archives and the University of California Berkeley Ethnic Studies Library who safeguard our histories of resistance; to the visionary fellows and research apprentices of the Critical Perspectives on Democracy + Media Lab and The Tribunal Project who refuse the tyranny of the status quo; and to our friends at Eastwind Books of Berkeley, who keep our stories circulating—thank you for making this book possible.

The art exhibit and book publication is supported in part by the University of California Humanities Research Institute, with additional support by the Global Democracy Commons of the University of California, Berkeley Social Science Matrix, the Latinx Research Center, and the Department of Theater, Dance, and Performance Studies. We write this book in tribute to the organizers, scholars, students, and memory-workers who weave resistance into the fabric of daily life. With courage to imagine, to denounce, and to create a new world, bring on the tribunal. May it amplify the struggles now and yet to come.

Book art other than the artworks for the exhibit were designed by Eleni Berg, Javier Mateos-Campos, and Lulu Matute. The Tribunal Project logo is designed by Alison Xiong with Riley Bratsch and Lincoln Ruiz-Truong.

CATALOG OF ARTWORKS

The Art Exhibit Opening Reception
October 10th, 2025 | 5pm-7pm
Ethnic Studies Library
University of California, Berkeley

Art Exhibit Archivist and Curator Nathaniel Moore with Judith Talaugon
Assistant Curator Joaquin Min Antonio

PART ONE:
TRIBUNAL RISING

Introduction

Judith Talaugon and Angela Marino

This book is a movement response to the current conditions of genocide denial. It is written by a group of authors who bring shared experiences, reflections, and political analyses to uplift People's Tribunals as a living practice of collective truth-telling to hold perpetrators accountable for crimes against humanity. Unlike state "trials by ordeal"[1]—which are often deployed as tools of repression by those in power—People's Tribunals are public forums that assert collective truth when representation and justice are denied. They are not symbolic gestures or legal simulations; they are traditions of resistance and expressions of popular movement. Through public hearings, testimony, rallies, and ceremonial gatherings, people living under occupation and oppressive systems organize tribunals to reclaim memory, dignity, resistance, and justice.

Tribunal Rising was also written to commemorate the 1992 International Tribunal movement in the city of San Francisco to dismantle the legacy of Christopher Columbus and the Myth of Discovery.[2] In 1990, "[a]t the culmination of the Special International Tribunal on the Human Rights Violations of Political Prisoners and Prisoners of War in the U.S., the American Indian Movement extended a call to national liberation movements and anti-im-

---

[1] Congressional hearings that frontally attack academic freedoms are, as Scholar and writer, Nasmet Hawa states, "a modern equivalent of a trial by ordeal" noting that the trial by ordeal was "to exert control through fear and ritualized punishment," denying what Edward Said calls 'permission to narrate,' (July 31, 2025).

[2] The 1990 *Encuentro Continental de Pueblos Indígenas: 500 años de resistencia india y popular*, gathered more than 200 official delegates from Indigenous nations in Quito, Ecuador, following an Indigenous Uprising of thousands of people in June of the same year that shut the city down. The event included organizers of the International Treaty Council, to declare autonomous governance of Indigenous peoples as a prerogative and a right in the face of 500 years of struggle since the beginning of the colonial invasion. The Peace & Dignity Journeys also began at the 1990 Quito Encuentro continuing the long tradition of transcontinental prayer runs.

perialist allies, united by a shared vision of justice and equality. This vision emerged from a deep-seated commitment to human dignity and the elimination of age-old practices that perpetuate hatred and inflict both psychological and physical harm."[3] This statement by AIM formed the cornerstone for the Counter-Quincentennial Celebration and the activities that put the U.S. Federal Government on trial for its role in perpetuating the Doctrine of Discovery and its consequent crimes against humanity.[4]

The Doctrine of Discovery, issued on Columbus' second expedition in 1493, is written proof of stolen land with criminal intent: "should you fail to comply ['to the King and Queen of Spain as rulers of this land'] we assure you that with the help of God we shall use force against you, declaring war upon you from all sides and with all possible means." Reasserted into the U.S. legal system in 1823,[5] the Doctrine of Discovery became further embedded into the institutional development of Westward expansion.[6] Land grabs on the baseless claims of 'terra nullius' have yet to be returned. Moreover, from the Caribbean to the Pacific islands, institutional law was designed to deceive in such theft and violence: submit to the 'Highnesses,' or be subject to perpetual slavery, complete dispossession, and the guilt of your own subjugation.[7] As Franz Fanon so clearly saw in Algiers in 1961, such distortion is deadly to the psyche. Tribunals are one way to bring back truth and heal from the effects of chronic disinformation and harm.

In 1992, the Resistance 500 Coalition and Freedom Now Network[8] led by members of the American Indian Movement, New Afrikan Peoples Or-

3 The original text of this statement is part of the 1992 International Tribunal program and reprinted in this volume following the introduction.
4 Full statement follows in this volume on page 23.
5 Specifically the Doctrine of Discovery was cited in the 1823 U.S. Supreme Court decision, Johnson v. McIntosh. See Steven T. Newcomb, 2008; Nick Estes 2019, Deloria Jr. 1988.
6 Ibid. For more information see the Doctrine of Discovery Project at https://doctrineofdiscovery.org/.
7 The original text of the Papal Bull issued by Pope Alexander VI in 1493, Inter Caetera, Doctrine of Discovery reads: "we shall enslave your persons, wives and sons, sell you or dispose of you as the King sees fit; we shall seize your possessions and harm you as much as we can as disobedient and resisting vassals. And we declare you guilty of resulting deaths and injuries, exempting Their Highnesses of such guilt as well as ourselves and the gentlemen who accompany us."
8 This resistance finds its grounding in the relentless pursuit of our collective human rights, as embodied in United Nations Resolution 1514 XV, affirming the right to self-determination.

ganization, Puerto Rican/POW independence, Prairie Fire Organizing Committee (PFOC) (white anti-imperialists), Filipino, Queer Liberation, Chicano/Mexicano movements among many others organized the International Tribunal movement to come out en masse to shut down the quincentennial celebration.[9] The spark of this activism was the establishment of a national commission financed by U.S. congress ($1M), Texaco Corporation ($5M), and municipal public funds, to oversee a 20-city U.S. tour featuring replicas of Columbus' ships, the Niña, Pinta, and Santa Maria that would eventually, 'triumphantly," sail under the Golden Gate Bridge into San Francisco Bay on October 12, 1992.[10] In the lead up to the events, The 1992 International Tribunal of Indigenous and Oppressed Peoples in the USA with judges selected from the community and a formal 'trial and verdict' event held at Mission High School. Debates were held. Witnesses came forward. Testimonies were heard. Thousands of people gathered on the shores of the Aquatic Park in San Francisco to turn back the replica boats of Columbus. As co-author of this book and one of the movement leaders of the 1992 International Tribunal, Judy Talaugon stated, "Like the Tainos on Guanahani in 1492, we in the Bay Area saw Columbus coming at us and we had to deal with him."[11]

A gala of period-costumed actors in a mock-coronation ritual playing Columbus and Queen Isabella of Castile was disrupted with shouts and banners unfurling from the balcony at San Francisco City Hall. Lourdes Portillo released a brilliant short film satire featuring the theater company Culture Clash called *Columbus on Trial,* while performance artists Coco Fusco and Guillermo Gómez Peña toured the performance art piece, *Couple in the Cage: Two Amerindians Visit the West* (1992-93). Women Against Imperial-

9   In particular, as Alejandro Molina notes (in his essay in this volume) this leadership came from the American Indian Movement (AIM), New Afrikan Peoples Organization (NAPO), the Puerto Rican Independence movement, the National Committee to Free Puerto Rican POWs and Political Prisoners, the Movimiento de Liberación Nacional Mexicano, and Movimiento de Liberación Puertorriqueño, the Prairie Fire Organizing Committee, the May 19 Communist Organization, Malcolm X Grassroots Movement (MXGM), and the John Brown Anti-Klan Committee. Women Against Imperialism, and organizers of the Freedom Now National Network and Interfaith groups ranging from the National Council of Churches to the War Resisters League, also contributed.
10   Municipal budgets were also drawn to support these activities with resistance among activists. See John Curl, 2017.
11   Michael Arnold, "Protesters Stop Mock Landing of Columbus: Activism: Boat is turned away in San Francisco. Egg-thowing demonstrators disrupt parade; 40 arrested," *Los Angeles Times*, Oct 12, 1992.

ism created a massive quilt. Committees, often led by women, organized in schools, on the radio, on streets, and in theaters and community centers to advocate for the recuperation of stolen lands, the release of political prisoners, and access to education to serve peoples' rights to self-determination.[12]

Tribunals were organized from New York 1990, to San Francisco in 1992, and then to Hawai'i in 1993 with Dr Richard Kekuni Blaisdell, all with prisoner defense at the center in order to expose U.S. internal colonialism that sought to hide the existence of political prisoners and prisoners of war.[13] Each tribunal built on the next, from Columbus and the Counter-Quincentenary to the 1898 U.S. military overthrow of Hawai'i's Queen Lili'uokalani. Activists, artists, and movement leaders gathered through the tribunal to denounce the celebrations of genocide and bring new characterizations to the struggle against settler colonialism, systemic racism, and generational harm. They became the counter-celebration.

Rather than accepting Columbus's pageantry as innocuous 'apolitical' or even 'cultural' traditions,[14] the critique made by movement organizers in 1992 was grounded in the recognition that such 'scenarios of conquest' (Taylor 2003)[15] were actively contributing to a genocidal erasure. Dakota scholar Kim TallBear shows how this erasure works through "physical, social, economic, and regulatory engineering" (2023, 93). The genocide of Indigenous peoples from Africa to the Americas, beginning with land dispossession and 'permanent slavery,' continues to operate in and through modern-day scenarios of Crusader Wars. The sword bearing Saint George transferred readily from *Santiago matamoros* (moorslayer) in Spain to *Santiago mataindios*

12 Including Berkeley activists that established Indigenous Peoples' Day, see *Handbook for Activists and Document History*, 2017.

13 See Luis Alejandro Molina's 'snapshot' recollection of the 1990-1993 tribunals in this volume, reprinted with permission,from *Remaking Radicalism*, 2020.

14 *The Los Angeles Times* reported that Joseph Cervetto Jr. who played Columbus in full period costume during the 1992 city-sanctioned Columbus parade waved a sword from his float shouting "We'll do it every year—Columbus Day!" See Michael Arnold, *LA Times* Oct 12, 1992. Despite the fact that Columbus never set foot in North America and that Columbus's voyage was commissioned by Spain, not Italy, a right-wing faction of The Italian American Foundation continues to lobby policies that support the myth of Columbus in the name of 'cultural preservation.'

15 Performance studies scholar Diana Taylor (2003) describes the scenario as a 'culturally specific imaginary,' that is repeatedly performed over time in ways that transmit a ready-made plot and paradigm of meaning, in this case the racist assumption of European 'righteous' dominion.

(indian-killer) in Peru with the same scenario of the trampled 'infidel' under the hooves. Mexica-Izkaloteka activist, Tupac Enrique-Acosta, called it when he said that such a scenario "has provided the pathological nature that normalizes what is the defamation of humanity and the institution of the crime against humanity, which is colonization and genocide."[16] What was handed down as 'civic' in these scenarios, valor and righteous order, in other words, was already an indoctrination. In forums such as the 1992 International Tribunal, like many others today, we are confronting a long history of indoctrination with the prerogative to be free of it. Without such clarity, denial multiplies and exerts its injurious effects on daily life.

As the United States reaches 250 years of its own 'independence,' we find ourselves at a new precipice. The brutal nature of imperialism that we are witnessing today shakes the root systems of all peoples around the world. Its fault lines are the supply chains of weaponry and information linking repression at home to the war economy. In *Border & Rule* (2021), Canadian activist and writer, Harsha Walia states that "The never-ending war on terror, more accurately described as a war *of* terror, seamlessly integrated domestic immigration policy into overseas military operations" (Walia 55). Current violations of human and planetary life—including torture, starvation, displacement, genocide, and ecocide—are fueled by the weapons of U.S. military supplies such as General Dynamics, Caterpillar, Lockheed Martin, Raytheon, Palantir, and Boeing, with profits subsidized by U.S. tax dollars.

In anticipation of the 250th 'celebrations,' the 1992 International Tribunal provides the context in which today's genocidal escalations can be understood: the reality that today's U.S. empire is the bitter fruit of the Doctrine of Discovery,[17] settler colonialism, and slavery that continues in multiple forms, aiming to exterminate all life with Earth. A delegation of Haitian refugees in 1992, just after the coup of elected president Jean-Bertrand Aristide, knew this quite well. They carried the Haitian banner in the counter-Columbus rally in San Francisco, joining witnesses of all continents in collective defense.

16   See Tupac Enrique Acosta in *Mapping the Doctrine of Discovery*: podcast.doctrineofdiscovery.org. Tonatierra, 2022.
17   See *The Doctrine of Discovery: Unmasking the Domination Code*, a film directed by Sheldon Wolfchild (Dakota) and co-produced by Steven T. Newcomb (Shawnee, Lenape) premised on the book *Pagans in the Promised Land: Decoding the Doctrine of Christian Discovery* (2008).

The border as evidence of the bipartisan project of elimination

"We must remind ourselves that borders on this hemisphere are recent lines drawn by the claws of capitalism. Borders preserve an imbalance, favoring those who benefit from the misery of broken kinship."
—From the Forward of *Red Nation Rising*,
by Radmilla Cody and Brandon Benallie

On March 18, 1992, a U.S. Border Patrol officer opened fire on 25 to 30 undocumented immigrants as they were walking near the Nogales border (Lytle-Hernandez, 2010). They were unarmed. Today, ICE attacks in urban and rural parts of the U.S. escalate a disappearance campaign designed as an act of cruelty. Young children have been systematically removed from their parents. Border Patrol, militia, and rangers continue to openly murder, beat, and rape. Yet the response to border conditions by the two running party candidates in the last election was to perform a bipartisan contest over who could best promote xenophobic nationalism, one by law and the other by the sword. Fascists falsely equate ordinary people in dissent as so-called 'terrorists' in proportional relationship to the onslaught of state terror.

Who is the real terrorist in this scenario? In his book *Against War*, Nelson Maldonado Torres writes that "[u]nlike Eurocentrism, which pursues expansion through the idea of the universal, Americanism fulfills a twofold role in the age of war against terror: it resists 'barbarians' from the inside and the outside simultaneously" (2008, 252). Rather than only at the U.S./Mexico border, such deadly fantasies, as *Red Nation Rising* authors describe, "exist everywhere settler order confronts Native order" (2021). As a line of confrontation between 'savagery and civilization,'[18] the bordertown extends well into the heart of the settler state, where "every town is a bordertown because every town serves as a border that settlers must defend." Bordertowns, in this analysis, are "meant not only to contain 'off the reservation' Indians, but to prevent Black relatives and other enslaved human beings from seeking

---

18   Like 'civilization vs barbarism,' this term was popularized in 19th century discourse, including famously by historian Frederick Jackson Turner's Frontier Thesis (1893) as cited in *Red Nation Rising* (2021).

refuge within Native societies." In this way, border towns are the ground zero of genocide, where we can see the tensions within border town institutions escalated by federalism in its attempt to shore up and reconstitute (united) state power. We are reminded of fantasies of 'defense' being played out in psychological projection. Like the Doctrine reads, it is a pathological reversal of reality itself.

For two hundred and fifty years, the U.S. has heavily invested in controlling its imperial frontiers wherever this scenario of crusaders may be imagined and engaged, in city streets, towns, forests, and schools. Not least, it manifests in policies driven by the need for profit through extraction, mining, and bodily labor exploitation. The result is not surprising. Like frontier military supply forts turned into prisons, detention centers for profit sprang into the borderlands, now the swamps. Work-camp prisons-for-hire like CECOT in El Salvador supply the sadistic 'demand' of permanent containment. Of course we know that this is a manufactured demand by those in power. But it is an extension, as Ruthie Gilmore argues, of a carceral geography, including a 12-mile strip surrounding the circumference of the U.S. territorial border that has become a federally-designated capture and kill zone keeping people in as much as out. Just as war crimes are blasted over the media as spectacle, the arguments of children, scholars, carpenters, and neighbors are erased from view. Tribunals push back against this erasure and towards a renewed story of truth in testimonial evidence and collective witness.

A generation after the 1992 International Tribunal, we gather with the growing global movement against U.S. war crimes, illegal occupation, and genocide of Indigenous peoples of the world in Palestine, the Sudan, Myanmar, and in Abya Yala. In this gravity of despair, tribunals like the Spirit of Mandela and the UC People's Tribunal for Palestine offer a space to move steadily onwards to name the truth, and to make room for the coming accountability in a way that recognizes our local relationships to internationalism.[19] The UC People's Tribunal for Palestine notes that "[i]n general, people's tribunals draw their mandate from the 1976 Universal Declaration of the Rights of Peoples, which was adopted in Algiers as part of a non-aligned

19 See ucpeoplestribunal.org; spiritofmandela.org; and tribunalproject.org respectively on these projects. This volume for more on the Tribunal Project. See Gregg Castro on Native-led curriculum addressing the California Missions, 2021.

Third Worldist struggle for self-determination against imperialism."[20]

Now more than ever, People's tribunals act as an alternative to failed courts of justice and political representation in the heart of U.S. imperialism. New Afrikan freedom fighter, Shaka Shakur, spells it out most clearly in his essay following this introduction, "Tribunals created and operated by genuine representatives of the people are designed to construct a legal context and draw upon the power of the people to bring to justice those in power who commit crimes against them." By organizing to hold the power system accountable, we, as ordinary people, build our own collective power, a dual power grounded in the shared principles of our humanity. When the law fails, the tribunals rise.

As working groups of the Critical Perspectives on Democracy + Media Lab (D+M Lab),[21] we were well aware of the systemic and contradictory discourse of democracy that served as a shield for U.S. intervention in the Americas and the world. We also saw solidarity organizations and academics over decades readily disposed to critique dictatorship elsewhere, but sometimes less inclined to confront it at home or, moreover, to recognize that it is possible to rethink the idea of united states altogether. So we began by first asking questions internal to the U.S.: how can a society be democratic while being so highly unequal, systematically unjust, and hyper-militarized? In 2014, a Princeton study of 1,800 institutions and organizations in the U.S. was published in which researchers concluded that a ruling class steers the country's political choices regardless of the will of a majority.[22] Rather than a representative democracy, their research found that the country was functioning more as an oligarchy than a democracy. Such a system removes ethical choice since it operates on the coercive influence of internal colonialism as much as an unethical dependency on ruinous forms of extraction, killing, and corruption.

Guyanese historian Walter Rodney wrote, "...[T]he colonial situation is

---

20 See ucpeoplestribunal.org
21 The Critical Perspectives on Democracy + Media in the Americas Lab (D+M Lab) is a UC Berkeley-based faculty initiative founded in 2017 that brings together scholars and community partners to address critical contradictions in the terms of democracy within the Americas of Abya Yala. We focus on the intersections of popular education, media, policy, and performance studies. demoxmedia.org
22 See Martin Gilens and Benjamin I. Page, 2014.

antithetical to any form of democracy—even to bourgeois democracy" (2022, 137).[23] The simple truth of this statement is to ask, how can the people rule if they are colonized? Likewise with the extraordinary imbalance of world military powers. If military repression or disinformation is the only way to hold power, then that power is not given by choice. For this reason, we reject the premise that democracy and imperialism are compatible. Moreover, as the president of Brazil, Luis Inácio Lula da Silva, has stated, "democracy is not simply the right to vote in an election. It is the right to participate in the decisions of the government." While nominal elections occur in the U.S., evidence shows that ordinary people as protagonists of change are systematically eliminated from any meaningful part of the democratic process.

This book features at its center a collection of reflection essays about specific documents that came from the 1992 organizing efforts in an exhibit at the Ethnic Studies Library on the UC Berkeley campus. Among them are the program and verdict of the 1992 International Tribunal of Indigenous Peoples and Oppressed Nations in the USA, which was held at Mission High School on October 3rd through 5th of that year, artworks and pamphlets, statements, and curricula such as the *Rethinking Columbus* publication that sold more than 300,000 copies of the first volume. Part Two of the book also serves as a reflection of living memories from a panel of speakers called 1992: Liberation Struggles Past and Present.[24] The panel featured co-author Judy Talaugon of the 1992 Tribunal, Arthur League of the Los Angeles chapter of the Black Panther Party, and Claude Marks, journalist and co-founder of the Freedom Archives. These reflection essays at the *mero medio* offer important perspectives on lessons learned through the writings of a new generation, most of whom were born after the millennium. Former D+M Lab graduate fellow, Destina Bermejo, calls this process "intergenerational decolonial pedagogies" to describe ways that youth with elders learn and share with experiential consciousness and dialogue at the heart of their work.

Part Three of this volume includes two chapters: the first, to undo the ill-logics of imperialism through research and critique, and the second, to

23 Walter Rodney, *Decolonial Marxism*, Verso 2022.
24 The exhibit is in collaboration with the Freedom Archives, which houses video and print materials primarily from the 1960s to the 1990s.
See freedomarchives.org.

decolonize the principles of democracy for our long-term futures. In the first chapter, Lulu Matute, Coordinator of the School of the Americas Watch (SOA Watch), with the support of a team of researchers, documented the 2022 indictment and conviction of the former president of Honduras, Juan Orlando Hernandez (JOH). This chapter, "The U.S.-Making of a Narco State," traces the decade-long symbiotic relationship between Juan Orlando Hernández (JOH) and U.S. officials—a partnership that endured until his conviction for international drug trafficking. It examines how U.S. actors, including Secretary of State Hillary Clinton, first legitimized the 2009 coup against democratically elected President Manuel Zelaya, then enabled JOH's illegitimate rise and unconstitutional rule.

At a time when the U.S. has eight war ships pointing at the people of Venezuela in a preposterous claim that Maduro is a part of a fictional cartel, a narrative entirely constructed by Marco Rubio and the White House to invade the Caribbean oil-rich nation, the analysis exposes Washington's operations of hybrid warfare. While aggressively sanctioning and bounty hunting Venezuela over baseless narcotics charges, U.S. officials were openly cooperating with Hernández who was indicted for the same charge. Why are they silent about Uribe, about Hernández, or about their relationship to arms dealing in Haiti? The pattern is unmistakable—Global North powers destabilize democracies, then obscure their complicity. Meanwhile, the human costs were catastrophic, causing mass exodus and land dispossession. Yet with Xiomara Castro's election, this chapter also documents Honduras' ongoing struggle to reclaim sovereignty from the wreckage of imperial impunity—what Ngũgĩ wa Thiong'o calls "the den of thieves."

In the final chapter, we turn from the work of the tribunal to confront imperialism with methods of decolonizing political cultures. In this chapter, Felipe Beleje Kan and Javier Mateos-Campos describe what they call Dialogues of Knowledge, which was a practice activated among Maya communities in Guatemala in 2023 to defend themselves from dictatorship, and uphold the election results in favor of the president, Bernardo Arévalo. After continual attempts to discredit and disqualify the national elections by interests allied with the former genocidal dictator Ríos Montt, this defense was in part made possible through the genuine participatory consensus-building of the Maya

Dialogues. Kan and Mateos-Campos describe this spiral form dialectic with adaptations for multilingual talking circles in the Maya diaspora.

The Maya dialectics, or as Gloria Chacón calls them, 'cosmolectics,'[25] deepen the *buenvivir* and *sumak kawsay* as political practice to reconstitute the principles of well-being in balance, dignity, and fulfillment. To live well in this sense is not about maximizing luxurious accumulation. It is about stewardship, weaving, and relationship with Earth as our common mother. What brings this framework together is valuing and integrating the revolutionary experience of resistance in the global South with those in the North. Following the important question posed by authors of the book, *What Kind of Ancestor Do You Want to Be?*, this chapter asks, what can we continue, and how do we endure? We can thus learn from each other, share tools, and organize with a regional anti-imperialist alliance that stretches the entire Pacific Coast of Abya Yala.

The work of this book seeks to uplift the harmonious and abundant ways that we can transform existing political systems, next to the longstanding arguments against colonial repression of land, the body, and the psyche. We are aware that genocide is the product of a fascism that has long been here in the heart of the U.S. empire. Its intended effects are to stun, to shake us in its wake, to silence, and to kill. Americanism displays a thunderous and spectacular evil that throws white phosphorus on skin, while drone anvils destroy people's homes from the sky. Why would we want to seek inclusion into an empire of terror? Robotic dogs with claw-like hind legs designed to patrol rugged terrain turn our university laboratories into dystopian science fiction factories.[26] Will these machines be programmed to deliver water in the desert, or will they hunt down, surveil, and kill? Perhaps both. We once again turn to the tribunal to reject assault in the name of 'innovation,' and to question 'discovery' within a system still operating within its Doctrine. These are not conspiratorial fears, it is a serious critique that stems from the very hauntings of the settler colonial state that refuses contrition, and continues to perpetrate with impunity, hostility, and injury. For this reason, our work is

---

25 See Chacón, 2018.
26 Since the early 1500s, canine attack forces have been notorious in many parts of the world as a lethal weapon used against Black and Indigenous people of the Americas.

dedicated to the vital return of ancestral remains, the demilitarization of our campuses, and liberation principles within all of our studies.

By reactivating the legacy of the 1992 Tribunal, our scholarship claims our sovereign rights as a people to live free from terror in our neighborhoods, in our classrooms, and around the world. What we offer in this volume is but a drop in an ocean of abolition, a small collection of documents, posters, and art that is part of the work of grassroots movement-building that brought Christopher Columbus and the colonial legacy of 'discovery' to trial in the United States. In the People's tribunal, the arts in song, theater, poetry, and print are forms of expressive evidence and a vital method of truth-telling.[27] These works brought mass collective action and policy changes. Columbus' obsolescence today is a movement victory towards next phase revolutionary work to dismantle the hardware of imperialism.

The final section of this book is a limited appendix of People's Tribunals. It does not pretend to be a comprehensive review. Rather it presents a few different examples from a wide range; some are global in scope or scale, others more specific in their impact. Tribunals often start as campaigns that lead to more formal proceedings. Notably many of the tribunals in the appendix focus on genocide taking place in Gaza, which is considered 'the compass' for revolutionary movements and what many activists call 'a litmus test for humanity.'[28] Tribunals that promise to hold accountability despite decades of (cynical) impunity raise the crucial questions of the role of enforcement. What would a global movement to enforce peace and the right of all Indigenous peoples to return to their homelands look like today? How might People's Tribunals provide a space to recognize the sovereign rights for self defense? Thanks to Dayani Albuquerque, whose research kick-started this project, the appendix is offered to expand the possibilities of future study.

Tribunal Rising serves as a reminder that we are interconnected in the counter-celebration from small towns to cities, from collectives to libraries

---

27 To perform is to bring forth, to assert the life energy of ollin, even if just a glimpse, it is the energy of the universe that moves through us, "the vibrant being" is life to heal (Valdez 2021). To perform is inherently an act to create, to regenerate. In this way, Tribunal Rising upholds the movement for justice including performance in the Peoples' tribunals.

28 See the People's Conference for Palestine 2025, peoplesconferenceforpalestine.org.

and schools that are engaged in popular education, housing, and health justice, restoring plants and waterways, food sources, and the right to live in a true zone of peace.

About the exhibit

Part Two of this book is dedicated to a collection of documents and images that are part of an art exhibit held at the UC Berkeley Ethnic Studies Library in Fall 2025. The exhibit is curated by the Tribunal Project in collaboration with the D+M Lab and the Ethnic Studies Library, Nathaniel Moore, with curatorial assistance from Joaquin Min Antonio. Archival materials were selected from collections housed at the Ethnic Studies Library and The Freedom Archives (freedomarchives.org) thanks in part to a planning grant by the University of California Humanities Research Institute. Reflection essays accompany each of these works to serve as a companion catalog.

The exhibit planning included a panel entitled 1992: Liberation Struggles Past and Present held in Fall 2024, featuring Judy Talaugon, Arthur League, and Claude Marks as speakers. The panel provided a chance to learn more about the personal journey of community leaders. It was organized by Seth Donnelly and recorded by Javier Mateos-Campos and Priscilla Vasquez.

There can be no stronger partner in this struggle than that of the Freedom Archives, a mighty vault of memory for people to recuperate information too often broken by these many fronts of imperialist assault. A special thanks to Claude Marks and Nathaniel Moore, whose expertise and generosity in shar-ing between these two collections provide a model for community partner-ship. In small groups, speaker series, and the media productions of the D+M Lab (2022-2024), we are proud to partner with the Freedom Archives and the Ethnic Studies Library in highlighting the 1992 International Tribunal move-ment, which include some of the formal documents of the Tribunal event, as well as movement pieces that highlight major issues during that period in the Bay Area. Together, with inspiration from the materials and organizer's stories from 1992 and other tribunals that are rising as we speak, we present these selected works and writings to uphold the formation of co-existence, trust, and the making of a bold and abundant path to liberation.

About the Tribunal Project

The Tribunal Project, led by Judith Talaugon, was one of four working groups of the D+M Lab in 2023-2025 that included weekly meetings and many conversations with Judy with her 'young mentors' including Destina Bermejo, Riley Bratsch, Katherine Garcia, Sarai Melendez, Joaquin Min Antonio, Jason Munguia, Alexander Quiroz, Leslie Ramirez, Abby Román, Carlos M. Santana, Alison Xiong, and many more.

#VoicesSetFree includes the recording and archiving of oral histories to carry truths of our times forward to future generations. The Tribunal Project continues in social media and planning for an upcoming tribunal on the California Missions. See **tribunalproject.org** and a statement of the Tribunal Project in this volume.

Works Cited

Acosta, Tupac Enrique. "The Doctrine of Discovery in the Context of Abya Yala with Tupac Enrique Acosta" in *Mapping the Doctrine of Discovery*, S1E05, 20 Oct 2022, (last accessed August2024). https://podcast.doctrineofdiscovery.org/assets/pdfs/Episode-05-Doctrine-of-Discovery-Abya-Yala-Tupac-Enrique-Acosta.pdf

American Indian Movement. Verdict of the International Tribunal of Indigenous Peoples and Oppressed Nations in the USA. San Francisco: 1992. www.freedomarchives.org/Documents/Finder/DOC35_scans/35.1992tribunal.verdict.english.pdf

Castro, Gregg. "California Missions in the California Indian History Curriculum," in *Telling and Teaching the Truth of the California Missions: Transforming Classrooms, Museums, and State Parks*. Critical Mission Studies. September 20, 2021. YouTube video, 1:24:09. https://www.youtube.com/watch?v=mN1molzyei4.

Chacón, Gloria Elizabeth. *Indigenous Cosmolectics: Kab'awil and the Making of Maya and Zapotec Literatures*. North Carolina UP, 2018.

Curl, John (as curator) *Indigenous Peoples Day: A Handbook for Activists & Documentary History*. CreateSpace Independent Publishing Platform, 2017.

Debord, Guy. *The Society of the Spectacle*. 1967. Zone Books, 1994.

Deloria Jr., Vine. *Custer Died for Your Sins: An Indian Manifesto*. UP Oklahoma, 1988.

Estes, Nick. *Our History is the Future: Standing Rock versus the Dakota Access Pipeline and the Long Tradition of Indigenous Resistance*. Verso, 2019.

Estes, Nick and Melanie Yazzie, Jennifer Nez Denetdale, and David Correia. *Red Nation Rising: From Bordertown Violence to Native Liberation*. PM Press, 2021.

Fanon, Franz. *The Wretched of the Earth [1961]*. Grove Press, 2007.

Gilens, Martin, and Benjamin I. Page. "Testing Theories of American Politics: Elites, Interest Groups, and Average Citizens." *Perspectives on Politics* 12, no. 3 (2014): 564–81. https://doi.org/10.1017/S1537592714001595.

Gilmore, Ruth Wilson. *Golden Gulag: Prisons, Surplus, Crisis, and Opposition in Globalizing California*. UC Press, 2007.

Hausdoerffer, John and Brooke Parry Hecht, Melissa K. Nelson, and Katherine Kassour Cummings, Eds. *What Kind of Ancestor Do You Want to Be?* University of Chicago Press, 2021.

Hernández, Kelly Lytle. *Migra!: A History of the U.S. Border Patrol.* University of California Press, 2010.

Hernández, Roberto. *Coloniality on the US/Mexico Border: Power, Violence, and the Decolonial Imperative.* University of Arizona Press, 2019.

Maldonado Torres, Nelson. *Against War: Views from the Underside of Modernity.* Duke UP, 2008.

Molina, Luis Alejandro. "International Tribunals for Self-Determination, 1990-1993," in Remaking Radicalism: *A Grassroots Documentary Reader of the United States*, 1973-2001, Eds Dan Berger and Emily Hobson. University of Georgia Press, 2020: p. 451-2.

Newcomb, Steven T. *Pagans in the Promised Land: Decoding the Doctrine of Christian Discovery.* Fulcrum Publishing, 2008.

Prashad, Vijay. *Hyper-Imperialism: A Dangerous, Decadent New Stage.* Tricontinental: Institute for Social Research (Dossier), 23 Jan 2024.

Quijano, Aníbal, and Michael Ennis. "Coloniality of Power, Eurocentrism, and Latin America." *Nepantla: Views from South*, vol. 1, no. 3, 2000, pp. 533–580. *Project MUSE*, https://muse.jhu.edu/article/23906.

Risling-Baldy, Cutcha. *We Are Dancing for You: Native Feminisms and the Revitalization of Women's Coming of Age Ceremonies.* University of Washington Press, 2018.

Red Nation. *The Red Deal: Indigenous Action to Save Our Earth.* Brooklyn, New York: Common Notions, 2021.

Rodney, Walter. *Decolonial Marxism: Essays from the Pan-African Revolution.* London: Verso, 2022.

Shakur, Shaka. "The New Modern-Day Militarized Fort!" *CounterPunch,* 26 Mar. 2024, https://www.counterpunch.org/2024/03/26/the-new-modern-day-militarized-fort/.

TallBear, Kim. "Indigenous Genocide and Reanimation, Settler Apocalypse and Hope." *Aboriginal Policy Studies* (Edmonton, Alberta, Canada) 10, no. 2, 93-111 (2023).

Taylor, Diana. *The Archive and the Repertoire.* Duke UP, 2003.

United Nations, Human Rights Council. *Anatomy of a Genocide: Report of the Special Rapporteur on the situation of human rights in the Palestinian territories occupied since 1967*, Francesca Albanese. March 25, 2024.

Walia, Harsha. *Border & Rule: Global Migration, Capitalism, and the Rise of Racist Nationalism.* Chicago: Haymarket Books, 2021.

The Tribunal as Anti-Imperialist Action

Shaka Shakur

TRIBUNAL | noun

1. A seat or court of justice.
2. The platform or seat upon which a judge or other presiding officer sits in court.
3. Anything having the power of determining or judging: the tribunal of public opinion.

[Latin tribunal — court of the tribunes; from tribunalis, of a tribune; from tribunus, TRIBUNE.]

To what judicious body shall the colonized man or womyn appeal for justice and freedom—justice untainted by the fingertips and intrusion of imperialism, which tips the scale forever in its favor? What judicious body serves the interest of the oppressed, the neo colonized, who is more than just that of a paper tiger?

Tribunals are intended to be impartial forums that serve both the people and the ends of justice. Yet, they often lack the power to enforce their findings. For the oppressed or colonized, the decision to pursue a tribunal is both a strategic and tactical one—an avenue not only to air our grievances, but to charge the oppressor, such as the U.S. government, with crimes like genocide.

This approach—strategically and tactically—exposes the hypocrisy of the naked State. It reveals the crimes and inhumanity of the State and seeks to strip away its legitimacy and prestige while simultaneously politicizing and educating the people.

Tribunals created and operated by genuine representatives of the people are designed to construct a legal context and draw upon the power of the people to bring to justice those in power who commit crimes against them. These crimes include not only violent acts, but also the creation of corrupt and oppressive policies that uphold repressive regimes and governments. Politicians and officials claim to serve the people—our people. Shouldn't the people, then, have the right to hold them accountable when they betray the public trust or the will of the masses?

Should the people not be empowered to form their own tribunals and courts to put tyrannical oppressors on trial? And should not these findings, through a revolutionary process, be enforced by bodies that truly represent the people—rather than relying on institutions that claim to serve the down-trodden but are financed by the very governments and entities responsible for their suffering? These institutions are not only undemocratic—they are a farce.

One historic example of engaging such undemocratic bodies is the 1951 petition submitted to the United Nations by William Patterson, titled "We Charge Genocide," which indicted the United States government for crimes against its Black population.[1]

More recently, a People's Tribunal was organized by The Spirit of Mandela coalition, led by Jalil Muntaqim, and held in New York State.[2] A panel of international jurists and respected judges presided. The United States was not only indicted for crimes against humanity—it was found guilty for its systemic and genocidal acts against African and New Afrikan people.

This is one form of Tribunal, in which national liberation movements and revolutionary forces bring forth evidence and charges against a colonial or neo-colonial power—in this case, the U.S.—under the framework of international law.

Another powerful example is The People's Tribunal on Jails and Prisons, organized in Richmond, Virginia by The Defender in collaboration with other grassroots organizations. This Tribunal put the Virginia Department of Corrections on trial and, with testimony from a cross-section of the community and legal experts, found it guilty of violating the human rights of incarcerated

1   William Patterson's petition to the United Nations, "We Charge Genocide," was submitted in 1951.
2   See the "Spirit of Mandela" website to learn more about the Tribunal held in New York, spiritofmandela.org.

people. The findings were submitted to the state legislature, the media, and other relevant bodies.

Historically, tribunals have allowed indigenous and colonized communities to both mobilize and empower themselves, offering a platform to speak truth to power. They enable us to organize independently and bring legitimacy to our struggles—broadening and deepening our movements as we build networks and alliances against a common foe.

Capitalism and imperialism recognize no borders and care nothing for so-called race. They will exploit the labor of even an ant if they can profit from it. There is intersectionality among all oppressed peoples—whether their struggle is rooted in class, in national liberation, or both.

We Are Our Own Liberators

So, what role do Tribunals play in an era marked by the rise of figures like Donald Trump, the realignment of global superpowers, and the resurgence of open imperialism? Especially when the U.N. Security Council is controlled by war criminals with veto power, blocking any resolution with teeth? When the International Criminal Court can indict a war criminal like Netanyahu, and the world merely shrugs? When people—womyn, children, the elderly—are being slaughtered in Palestine, Sudan, Haiti, the Congo, and yet these international bodies remain impotent? What, then, is the role of People's Tribunals in this era?

People's Tribunals must be weaponized by the people and geared toward their mobilization. We do not require approval or validation from official bodies to legitimize our struggle. We are not begging to be rescued. Instead, we use tribunals tactically—placing our findings into public and international arenas to help cultivate the conditions necessary for a revolutionary process, a Vita Wa Watu—a life for the people.

We organize to build dual power and develop the terrain of People's Power. This is not rhetorical—it is part of a scientific and dialectical process.

The practice of organizing tribunals helps us create liberated space— where we can connect with other movements, activists, and revolutionaries.

It gives us room to bridge gaps, engage in ideological struggle, build strategic alliances, and form principled working relationships. Through these efforts, we expose and name the real enemies of the people—and of humanity as a whole.

We have never needed the State—or any government body—to validate our struggles. It is the height of hypocrisy and political suicide to let those you rightly identify as your oppressors dictate the rules of engagement.

We legitimize our own struggle by taking our issues directly to the people, creating venues for truth, justice, and revolutionary accountability. Through these people's forums, we raise our voices in righteous anger and serve notice to our oppressors—by word and by deed—Your time is up. The End.

Shaka Shakur is a New Afrikan political prisoner currently being held in Virginia. For more information on Shaka's campaign for freedom and other writings, see the full bio on the contributor's page and www.shakashakur.org.

Dismantling the Legacy of Columbus:
The Origins of the International Tribunal and
the Counter-Quincentennial Movement[1]

At the culmination of the Special International Tribunal on the Human Rights Violations of Political Prisoners and Prisoners of War in the U.S. in December 1990, the American Indian Movement extended a call to national liberation movements and anti-imperialist allies, united by a shared vision of justice and equality. This vision emerged from a deep-seated commitment to human dignity and the elimination of age-old practices that perpetuate hatred and inflict both psychological and physical harm. Within this framework lies our commitment to education, advocacy, and resistance in the lead-up to the quincentennial commemorations, fostering a shared platform for celebration and future collaboration on issues of mutual concern.

This call formed the cornerstone for the Counter-Quincentennial Celebration and the activities encapsulated within the International Tribunal, Civil Disobedience Demonstrations, Marches, Rallies, and more. We emphasize "celebration" because our endeavor to organize this Tribunal is rooted in the celebration of resistance against genocide, colonialism, and political oppression. This resistance finds its grounding in the relentless pursuit of our collective human rights, as embodied in United Nations Resolution 1514 XV, affirming the right to self-determination. We strive to forge our destinies and construct our futures, leveraging the rich tapestry of human and natural resources that rightfully belong to us.

---

1 This statement was frequently read by Judy Talaugon of the 1992 Tribunal, and is additionally documented as a statement in the Indigneous Peoples Day: A Handbook for Activists & Documentary History curated by John Curl (2017).

Nearly two years have passed since the inception of this journey, marked by enriching and respectful dialogues. In this time, we have achieved a modest yet crucial milestone, uniting diverse sectors around three core principles:

Demystifying Columbus: In 1992, we vowed to ensure that the "big lie" never again takes contemporary forms, challenging notions of white cultural, racial, and genetic superiority. Our aim is to dispel the myths surrounding Columbus and his legacy.

Self-Determination: The foundational principle of self-determination underpins many of today's global conflicts. The national movements represented here—Native American, New Afrikan (Black), Mexican, and Puerto Rican—all share a common history of being denied the fundamental power to shape their destinies. Our mission is to reclaim that power.

The Liberation of Political Prisoners/Prisoners of War: Across the world, the U.S. government has linked foreign aid and recognition to the release of political prisoners and POWs. Astonishingly, the U.S. stands alone among major powers in denying the existence of political prisoners and POWs within its borders. Currently, hundreds of individuals languish in captivity for political reasons related to their self-determination movements. Some have endured for nearly decades for crimes they did not commit. Others face virtual life sentences for political activities safeguarded by international covenants. We stand in solidarity to demand their freedom, ensuring their voices are heard and justice prevails.

For centuries, history has been penned by the conquerors, favoring the empire builders of Europe and later the United States. Today, we embark on a mission to rewrite this narrative, to dismantle the legacy of Columbus, and to reshape the course of history in the pursuit of justice, self-determination, and freedom for all oppressed peoples. Together, we commit to this noble endeavor.

.

An Interview with Comrade Judy Talaugon

Conducted by Seth Donnelly on October 24th, 2024

SD: It's an honor to be here today with Comrade Aunty Judy Taluagon. Talk about your background as an Indigenous activist both here in Sonoma and beyond.

JT: I am a California Native person. My father and I are tribal members of the Chumash Nation in Santa Ynez, California. I was born in Santa Barbara County, but I was raised here in Sonoma County. My village down there in Santa Ynez is the village of Kalawashaq. We are actually called the Samala people. I come from there. My relatives are there. We now have a casino economy and have made a tremendous contribution to the county of Santa Barbara. I'm very proud of my people.

At the same time, we have had to deal with the missile launchings that go on at Vandenberg Air Force base. Since forever, some of us have been opposed to these launchings. Even though we've been yielding to the military occupation of the Vandenberg Air Force base, some of us do not recognize this occupation as legitimate. I continue to join protest vigils organized by the Catholic Worker from Guadalupe. Guadalupe is 10 miles from Vandenberg Air Force Base. We see those missile tests, it's not a joke, it's frightening.

I'm the eldest of seven. My mother, who was Filipina, had a tremendous sense of justice. Both of my parents were engaged in a deep critique of U.S. society. My father and I are Californian Native people, meaning our history is deeply entangled with the Spanish Mission system. In California, everyone's life is entangled to a certain degree with the Spanish Mission system. By the fourth grade, you're taking a required history course in California, and it is specifically to do with the Spanish Missions and which has been used to define my people and the Kumeyaay, the Cahuilla and all Indigenous peoples who have been touched by the Spanish Mission system. It's very punitive. It's part of slavery and capture and land dispossession. My mother and father were not converts; they were always opposed to the Vatican and its Mission system.

When I was in high school, after my family moved to Sonoma, I began paying attention to the activists coming through our household, being there and providing coffee, meeting Indigenous activists involved in the occupation of Alcatraz, in the defense of the "los Siete" political prisoners from the Mis-sion District in SF, and so many other struggles. These activists and experienc-es educated me to the liberation struggle. I met activists during the bloody summer in Farmington, New Mexico, when houseless and abandoned elderly Indian men were being murdered. As a teenager, I participated in arriving and holding space in courtrooms to defend our people, our political prison-ers. How did it start for me? A lot of times, it was holding space in courtrooms and holding a space in the circle.

SD: And your mother was active in the farm workers organizing, too, right?

JT: So that was a big part of my growing up. Both my parents were farm workers, both asserting a level of self-determination. That was revolutionary, you know? So it was, class struggle was identified in our house, now that I really think about it. Mom was definitely in the midst of organizing with the likes of Larry Itlion, the famous Filipino farmworker organizer.

My mother was with the first generation of Filipina asserting, the dalaga, the young women who were born in the U.S. amongst the Filipino bache-lor society. At first, the U.S. government would only allow Filipino men to come to the U.S., to come here and do the hard, underpaid work. Because of the anti-miscegenation laws, it was illegal for our men to marry. Our men, our manong, ended up pretty much a massive society of bachelors. There are things that they had no consent in, you know. Our people came here as cheap labor or slave labor after the U.S. invaded and occupied the Philip-pines. We had no say on the laws, all of the anti-laws against Chinese, against Filipino, against Mexicanos, the Bracero labor and migration and labor laws, anti-naturalization laws continued.

So thank you for mentioning my mother, because she went on into the field of immigration rights in San Francisco with Sandigan and banded together with other folks in the labor movement against Blue Shield and on behalf of a Filipina Nurse, Emma Salazar.

SD: *What was it like for you going to high school after you moved to Sonoma?*

JT: You know, it was the late sixties. It was 1968. And I was a mod, very fashionista. I was really into being a Mod and London musicians such as Ciela Black and micro minis, and Mom dug it. I was with a young Mom, and Mom was a very beautiful fashionista as well. I'm just saying I was aspiring towards Mom, who really kind of looked like Sade. Yeah. You know, severe ponytail and just very Sade.

So I arrived in Sonoma, where people were still wearing poodle skirts, and I thought it was really quite handsome looking. But I missed the beat. You know, I didn't get it. And so I was excited to go to my first dance. And that was my orientation to Sonoma. A group of people who were with me then are still alive today. So they'll remain unnamed. But they came up to me and lifted the hem of my skirt and said, "Where's the rest of your dress?" So that was very, very rough. But I used my wit, and I used my Mom's particular strength to just ride it off. Rise above it. Hold your chin.

In a sense, I was quite sheltered. I mostly stayed with my family, keeping closely to my sisters. But we kind of had a lot of bravado and acted like we were sort of on top of it. On top of the horse. We had horses. And at the same time we were around so many activists coming through the house and so were very aware. And we could be rebellious.

I was almost expelled. Mom had to come in and stop the process. I was almost expelled for using the G- word, "genocide" in a report. I was a sophomore in Sonoma Valley High School and it must have been close to 1969. And I was talking about social and cultural genocide that was inflicted on Indigenous children and their families by the "Indian Industrial" boarding schools, the residential schools. I wrote about it. I used some information that I got from a Life magazine at the time. This didn't stop the school from trying to expel me. I was what? I was 14 years old at the time. And our teacher just called me in and told me that this was just unacceptable and that he was going to give this to the principal. It could be grounds for expulsion. I really didn't get it until my mother came walking into the school with raging, red eyes.

That's where I got so much of my political education, from my mother. She educated me in labor rights, basic human and civil liberties. Just the basics. Sometimes at the dinner table. And my mother or father, mostly mother, instilled into my consciousness what should be our basic rights– just given to us all. The problem is, you know, our basic rights were not being respected by the larger society. So we did have a walkout at Sonoma Valley High School. The Vietnam war was going on, and we weren't supposed to talk about it. And those of us who talked about it were targeted by the school administration, which sent a letter home to our families. This letter accused us of doing drugs. I would say 85% of my friends were targeted by this horrible letter. It resulted in kids being needlessly punished by their families, in being kicked out of the house.

This was a good time to talk about what was really happening in society. And to take bold action. Young people were freeing their minds and trying to revolutionize society. It was exciting. We came to see ourselves as part of a global struggle against colonialism, a struggle being waged by the Vietnamese and all colonized peoples, including those within the U.S. empire, a struggle for Third World liberation. This was a very exciting time. If you were a book reader, which we were in those days, we loved having a book of a philosopher or a poet tucked under our arms. We pretended that we really knew what we were doing, but it was part of aspiring to be pretty well read up on the issues and respectful of one another's positions. This included kids who were being drafted and going into Vietnam. It was all real for us. We were confronting the divisions and segregation and fractures in the larger community.

We knew that we lived in a segregated, imperialist country. We worked with that information and we created a liberation front, a Third World liberation front in essence. We formed kitchens and liberation schools. We didn't just crumble and retreat within ourselves, or silo out. We were definitely in the same events, the same gatherings. They were not always big parties and discos and at the club, no, no, no. We brought our families, our dogs, our Moms. We used community centers and high school auditoriums. We created new spaces as well. We combined our libations from the African liberation movement and the American Indian Movement with our drums and our stage. We really made an effort. Oftentimes, we knew nothing but that self-determination had to take front and center. The grassroots of it all– it was just beautiful.

We were growing out of brutality. Even back then, we were aware of the liberation struggle in Palestine. The great Black feminist poet June Jordan took a position. This gave us tons of courage at the time, you know. I really want to emphasize the bravery and courage I learned in those days from having to go out into action when you didn't know if you were going to live or not. People were being seriously injured and sometimes killed by the police in these demonstrations. At the time when you do these things, you realize that if I'm still here, if we're still here, then we're certain that there's a future.

When I am working with students and young mentors today, I can feel their hunger to bring this back, to rebuild the liberation front, to get together under the same roof. There's a calling to bring back the clarity and the willingness to forge those bonds of solidarity and not just pull inwards, to not gentrify. We have yet to uncover what that might be. It is an exciting time if we just humble ourselves to remember that the potential of liberation was nipped, cut down by counter-revolution, in my generation before it could reach its potential.

Did we know what we were doing then? No, I was actually 17 years old. I knew then that we didn't know. I really did. I saw it in the eyes of those who survived the protests at the Democratic National Convention in 1968, who survived the protests at the draft induction centers and the beatings at Ohio State, those kinds of beatings that kind of attack. I knew we didn't have to martyr ourselves much beyond that. It was a full-on attack on the children by the police and the system of power. And we saw this. We said 'they're a cannibal,' they're eating their own children.

SD: After high school, you went to San Francisco. Talk a little bit about that part of your life and how your activism in San Francisco led you to help organize the Tribunal in '92.

JT: By then, I had already been twice out on the road to New York and to the Akwesasne, an Indigenous liberation organization, where red wire was happening. I had gone to the Mohawk movement. When I got back to the Bay Area, I went to San Francisco State. The smoke was just clearing on campus from the student strikes with the Third World Liberation Front. It really was a beautiful time to have peer counselors who were born from the movement. They just cared about us first first-generation students. They would knock on your door, and they really make you go to school. This was 1971 now. We just now had the Equal Opportunity Program (EOP) on campus.

The EOP department was teaming with peer counselors, and I could name them all. They really had good principled concepts. My first gig came from interacting with these folks. People like Nesbitt Crutchfield, Shaki Bomani, and Danny Glover– he was not an actor yet! Again, these were people in the movement right then and there at the student strikes on the SF State campus before they became celebrities. And there was Ed Delacruz, who's no longer with us, but I get to name his name now. He is the one who gave me a gig in the South of Market Central City, where I was a social worker and advocate with the Youth Advocates Huckleberry House. This was serving young people on the run. As advocates, we were providing 24-hour crisis care. The greater number of the children knocking on the door were two-spirits. They were running from group brutalities. That was my work then. I loved it.

SD: Talk about the student strike at SF State and the Third World Liberation Front.

JT: I hope that we will always tell these stories in the right way, tell how it really was, how it was born, and how it was later usurped by the media and the system of power. We need to really look at what we were trying to create and how it was temporarily usurped, disconnected from subsequent generations. We need to look at all life, and that's part of my seminar examining all the uprisings from this period, how they connect to today, how they've all been redefined. What do we see when we look at the archival footage?

There were many, many voices that we were finding in ourselves and uncovering from the liberation movements in the larger society, from the Black Panther Party and American Indian Movement to anti-colonial revolutions throughout the "Third World." We were tapping into a spiritual and cultural heritage that had been untold and nearly erased by the colonizer. Unfortunately, in place of our people's true voices and histories, we had white supremacist anthropologists and archaeologists, what we call pothole diggers, you know, a lot of PhDs out there telling stories and fantasies of a master race. This needed to really come to a screeching halt.

There were actions in the larger society that inspired our actions on the campuses. I'm talking about the Indigenous liberation actions at Alcatraz and Mount Rushmore, and so many land back actions. As Indigenous people on Turtle Island, we have been the first prisoners of war in this country, and we continue to have our prisoners of war behind bars now. Free Leonard Peltier! I would argue that Indigenous land dispossession, eugenics, and every bit of the elimination program against my people in Turtle Island was a key catalyst for our efforts to revolutionize what was happening on the campuses.

The struggle against colonialism and domination has never ever been part of the instructions of the universities. So we began finding new ways to be participants as scholar activists in history, law, language, and so much more. Those intellectual realities are harsh, but we've become ever more effective in using international law to claim a mountain. We can do that, we can protect religious freedom and protect land and human bodies at the same breath. We need to teach people that we've been excluded from a lot of the conversations to protect the land and the body. Indigenous dialogue and Indigenous intellectual knowledge need to be incorporated. If not, we're gonna lose deeply.

SD: In that spirit, you played a huge role in the 1992 Tribunal out of the Bay Area. Talk about that massive project.

JT: In 1992, there was the international call to celebrate the quincentennial, the so-called "discovery of the New World" by Columbus, to celebrate the 500 years of domination and the Doctrine of Discovery. The entire colonial narrative was to be punctuated in 1992. Those of us in the American Indian Movement and other liberation movements across the U.S. empire and worldwide, we got wind of this of course, we saw that the party was about to burst. We had already been setting our sights on the UN and changing international law. So about this pending celebration of the quincentennial, we said, "You know, it would be silly if we sat around and let this happen." We didn't have the Internet yet, but we did have fax machines and old school phones, and so on, and a little bit of computer capacity. We really had to use some old-fashioned tactics, and we started to organize 2 ½, maybe 3 years, ahead of '92. We began to strategize, what would that look like? How do we counter a quincentennial that is marking 500 years of genocidal practices, 500 years of elimination and scarring of Mother Earth, 500 years of extraction of the Amazon, which is the lungs of Mother Earth?

As a people, desperate for the world to invite us into the conversations, we decided to keep doing what we had been doing since the 60s. We'll start to be the teachers and reframe the whole quincentennial. We brought together broad-based coalitions worldwide. Younger activists got involved, and it was an intergenerational project. We encouraged 500-year committees to begin chapters worldwide. And they did. 500 Years of Resistance, 500 Years of Celebration and Survival of Indigenous Peoples. Our aim was to bring liberation movements together in SF to put Columbus and colonialism and white supremacy on trial, to call for the release of the political prisoners from our movements, and assert our rights to self-determination. We organized popular education workshops out of Mission High School, did street protests, and held major events across the city as part of the Tribunal.

These were the themes and the activities. There was a motif. In those days, there was the gorgeous movement art cultivated from a stream of consciousness, cultivated from our liberation movements. We needed to come back around and needed to hold each other up again, you know? By this point, we'd been through the brutalities of the 80s under Reagan. It was a scam of a time with the War on Drugs. Our families were torn apart like you've never seen before. Families being split up—Child Protective Services was in their heyday. There was the expansion of "urban removal" during the 70s and 80s, of the removal of people of color from our urban communities, like the International Hotel, and there was gentrification. There were our political prisoners, people like Leonard Peltier from AIM, the Black Panthers, and the Puerto Rican Independence activists who had been locked up for more than a decade, some even two decades, by 1992.

We were going through all of this and saw it getting worse as the powers that be got ready to celebrate 500 years of "discovery." So it wasn't time to kick in, to give up. Within our movements, like the American Indian Movement, we had to struggle with patriarchy, but we worked it. It was rough. There was factionalization. But, at the end of the day, when I look at it now, and I've got some of our old cadre still in proximity to myself, we really did survive based on our capacity to survive prior to 1992. There had already been COINTELPRO and the FBI's secret war on our movements in the 1960s and 1970s. We survived. A lot of us had gone to prison, a lot of us had led a clandestine existence, and yet we were just coming back around.

So we were ready to take on the Quincentennial in 1992. We were also kind of archivists, making and documenting our own histories with our own street journalism and research. We had developed our own tangible mechanisms and apparatus for sustaining our own narratives, the truth. There were a lot of these different movements, including folks coming out of the Black liberation struggle and Puerto Rican movement, all working together to expose colonialism and call for the release of political prisoners. And we continue to fight for their release today.

With Leonard Peltier, he's 80 years old this year and has faced incarceration since 1976![1] We have been fighting for executive clemency. He is a target by the U.S. government and has been wrongfully convicted all of these

---

1 Leonard Peltier was born on September 12, 1944. He was incarcerated in 1976 and was released to home confinement in February 2025. This means he spent approximately 49 years in prison, and 61.25% of his life incarcerated. At the time of his release he was 80 years old. The commutation by Biden did not pardon Peltier, meaning he remains convicted of the original crimes, while his legal team continues to seek a full pardon. Some critics view the house arrest as a form of solitary confinement, which can be detrimental to his health and well-being, especially given his age. Peltier suffers from various ailments, including diabetes, hypertension, and partial blindness. His supporters argue that his access to medical care is inadequate under house arrest. Supporters like Peltier's lead lawyer, Jenipher Jones, argue that any form of detention is unlawful, and that he should be free to move within his community.

years. There's been admissions to who had participated in that shootout on the Pine Ridge Reservation in 1975 and who was responsible for the deaths of those two FBI agents.

Those of us working on the Tribunal in 1992, we were abolitionists; we did not believe in the prison-industrial complex. Critical Resistance grew out of this activism in 1992. So did the Prisoners' Activist Resource Center. A lot of young affinity organizers in the Tribunal went on to do beautiful, amazing anti-racist and personal work, to work with organizations like Roots Against War.

We were able to do really effective solidarity work. This meant allowing youth of color to convene themselves and be at the table as leaders and consistently not be discounted. They brought their leadership all the way in, as a matter of fact. They were, I'd say, well-organized; they had the cultural arm, the political arm, you know, the arm that would go to New Orleans in the middle of Katrina, you know, that would attend many of the hearings around the uprising during the Rodney King trials.

As a key organization to come out of this, Roots Against War was led by youth of color, and I don't remember that happening elsewhere during that time. It was a cool thing, because it wasn't like trying to be cool. It just was. I'm saying it was a good thing, organically accepted. And again, in the 90s, it all mixed with hip-hop and hardcore. San Francisco was the hotbed for hardcore. Underground punk rock, thrash metal, an invention, a creation practically from the Bay Area. Radio personalities, both KPFA and the radio shows, were together. Davey D was not doing Hard Knocks Radio yet, but there was crossover at so many levels, so much. And, you know, there was a lot of creativity in our grassroots media.

The Tribunal was a beautiful effort, but there were problems in our movements. What was the beef with some of the guys? At times, there was this sort of unhinged brotherhood that was behaving in ways that made us unsafe. And it was very hard for all of us to understand what was going on. There was factionalism. One guy wanted to own the property, the trademark, and the copyright for the Tribunal. This went against what we were trying to create, a place where we can really assemble as a group, debate or argue at the time, get to the root of it from there, and guarantee that it will always be something deeper or something very simple.

The sisters and the women, they kept it going. The femmes, and the strong lesbians, if you will, on all fronts at the time. It would be the Dykes on Bikes, Lipstick Lesbian, the bands... We're flanking the women who are left to lead, because the men were mad at each other about who was going to own the property. Yeah. We didn't know that that was the real division. That was a quiet storm, and the rest of us, of course, organically just continued to feed the people and move the people. The meetings were in SF, in the brick building on 19th and Capp, and in the East Bay.

So, you know, man, it was broad and gorgeous, huge. I got calls from New York, Santa Cruz, LA, UCLA, all campuses activated, all fax machines 24-7 just rolling. Yeah. Fax machines. Alejandro was the, you know, the man. He was the master of graphics and marketing, which is, at the time, it sounds creepy now, but at the time was gorgeous to have someone who gave us our own motif to identify ourselves, even to this day. If you, if the readers were to Google 1992 San Francisco Tribunal, anti-Columbus, any of those, you will find beautiful programs and graphic works. I thank Alejandro Molina for this.

SD: You are now working with new young activists, new young scholars, people here in the community in Sonoma Valley, as well as in New York and beyond, on a new Tribunal Project. Talk about this new Tribunal and how it particularly connects to people here in Sonoma County.

JT: I don't have enough time to talk about all the wonderful and amazing cousins and tribal relatives that came before me on this topic. As California Indian people, we all live with this history, and it's part of our conversation. There's a whole batch of educators, graduate work by Chumash people that comes way before me. So I just want to say that. What I've done is to reach out. I wanted to always engage. I also saw that there's not much time. We have 21 Missions under the control now of California State Parks. You can find it on their website for the 21st Mission, right here in Sonoma Valley.

These past two years, I've been working with and mentoring young scholars out of UC Berkeley, and even out east, in upstate New York. We've been researching the archives of the 1992 Tribunal and laying the foundation for a new Tribunal today. This new Tribunal involves creating teach-ins, other forms of popular education, publications, art, and protests across the Americas to once again put settler colonialism on trial and celebrate ongoing Indigenous resistance and survival. This time we are putting a particular focus on Sonoma Valley, right here, the birthplace of the settler colonial entity called "California." We want to transform this last 21st Mission into a Site of Conscience that will be recognized by UNESCO. We want to create a curriculum through this site that will engage college, high school, and middle school students in learning the real history here.

This Mission here, you know, was a gallows, a killing site. It represents mass graves for my Indian people, the roundups, and the resistance, by the way. This whole area represents a zone of exploitation of Chinese railroad workers, even the early Italian communities, and, of course slavery of African people. So why not take that deep, deep history of state-sanctioned atrocity after the Gold Rush? This history should not be erased. The humanities are already in trouble. As an area of study in our schools, Social Studies is in trouble. I think that we can use more Indigenous cultural resources and real history to redefine Social Studies.

We have made brilliant relationships with parts of the State Park Service. I just came from visiting the Wabanaki people up in Maine. They have achieved a beautiful relationship with an architectural firm that took one year of learning the correct protocol of how to work with tribes. Now, the Wabanaki and this firm have created this amazing architectural design that reflects the tribe. We're in a new day.

There are a lot of historians here in Sonoma Valley. I'm 72 now. I have been in Sonoma Valley for many, many years. And we've sort of winked at each other. We know where there are graves that are not marked and not spoken of. But we also need to talk about it. We hope to mark these graves. We need to identify these places for the traditional owners of Sonoma Valley. They are not easily with us because of the massacres and the bloodshed around the Mission here. The crimes of the nefarious players against the Indigenous people of this Valley—from Salvador Vallejo, General Vallejo's brother, to the settlers with the Bear Flag Revolt—these crimes have been covered up for far too long.

We're blessed to have traditional owners like Desiree Harp and Tek-Tek and Scott, and the Wappo coming in and participating in enhancing our stories at the Tribunal today. We're blessed, blessed, blessed. That gives me hope that we could take this Mission and make it a Site of Conscience. We could influence UNESCO on such matters. We can learn also as a community how human rights need to be revisited. I would love to see the community engaged in a very serious reassessment of international law and classification for genocide. The unmarked graves in our midst should be classified as evidence of genocide. It is just like the Truth Commission that investigated genocide in Guatemala, an investigation that involved forensic evidence and the repatriation of remains of a very specific people. Why are we confused about genocide?

I want this Site of Conscience here to generate more genocide scholarship, as well as beautiful thought and poetry, and archival work on the survival and resilience of humanity. Let's see it happen. And let's develop a curriculum with the high schools and the middle schools, even. And let's leverage this new awareness into ongoing demands around the land, around water control, and play it forward. Land Back in our lifetime.

You know, Desiree Harp, one of the traditional owners of Sonoma Valley and Napa, does teach young and old community members here. She offers more than just cultural enrichment, but also environmental sciences from an Indigenous perspective, bits and pieces of decision-making and process in that way. Why not have an eight-week outdoor experiential history lesson, you know, with biology and cosmology shared? This is a real proposal to come to Sonoma Valley.

SD: One last question, what, given all your decades of experience, would be a few lessons you could pass on to today's young generation who are trying to revolutionize things?

JT: One bottom line thing is that I think we don't get a lot of principles in our practice, in our daily practice, that are based on our moral core, an exercise, a song, a prayer, Tai Chi, you know. Something that brings us back into our breath, that brings us back into the rhythm of what we might believe to be the universe. Because people are often caught up in their own heads, that part of our practice grounded in our bodies can get ignored, overlooked.

But I would say that let's just try to remember. A daily practice of reciprocity. Let's try to remember that we're free, that our eyes are taking us somewhere, our feet are taking us. That, number one, I know it sounds so humble, but I really do believe that this very specific new generation is open to receiving. I know that they need to capture their breath. They need to own their origin stories. They are clamoring for more wisdom. This new generation ought to demand that of people.

It's okay not to know, to take leaves of absence and regain footing, breathing. I've had to take leaves of absence in my life in order to pace myself. By doing so, I've been able over the long haul to keep showing up, to make it to actions. I had to show up, and people needed me to sit with them and with their shawls and our fans. So sometimes, not often, you do have to take a leave and take that time to breathe and come back, back in stronger than before you left off.

I would also tell today's generation to make our prisoners of war, our political prisoners, our prisoners of conscience a thought in your everyday life. I'm at your service.

Judy Talaugon is Chumash and Filipina daughter of farmworker and is the founder of the Tribunal Project and one of the movement leaders of the 1992 International Tribunal in San Francisco. tribunalproject.org

Seth Donnelly is a long-time high school teacher, member of the Haiti Action Committee, and co-founder of Taxpayers Against Genocide (TAG). https:// www.taxpayersagainstgenocide.org/

International Tribunals for Self-Determination, 1990-1993[1]

Luis Alejandro Molina

Thanks to the vision and organizing focus of Puerto Rican sociologist, lawyer, and activist Luis Nieves Falcón, a coalition of Black, Native American, Mexican, and Puerto Rican organizations developed three international tribunals in the early 1990s. These tribunals aimed to strengthen solidarity among antiracist and anticolonial organizations in the U.S., and to place them within the framework of international human rights.

The initial effort was the Special International Tribunal on the Human Rights Violations of Political Prisoners and Prisoners of War in the United States, held at Hunter College in December 1990. More than eighty-eight organizations across the U.S. dissident spectrum, from pacifist Catholics to groups that explicitly defined themselves as national liberation movements, worked together for over a year to produce an internationally recognized public forum. Organizers modeled the event on two tribunals earlier organized by British philosopher and activist Bertrand Russell, the first of which brought to light U.S. war crimes against the people of Vietnam. The 1990 tribunal highlighted the human rights abuses visited on more than one hundred "political prisoners and prisoners of war" in the United States. These people, all members of movements that had been targeted and repressed by the FBI's counterintelligence program, faced unduly harsh sentences even as the U.S. government denied the political nature of their incarceration and many progressive activists gave them little support. The following two tribunals, in 1992 and 1993, addressed issues of settler colonialism and Hawaiian sovereignty.

Each of the tribunals worked with renowned human rights attorneys and

---

1 Reprinted with permission from the author. Original text appears in *Remaking Radicalism: A Grassroots Documentary Reader of the United States, 1973-2001*, Eds Dan Berger and Emily Hobson. University of Georgia Press, 2020: p. 451-2.

presented a bill of charges against the U.S. government. Yet the success of the tribunal strategy was not juridical. Rather, success was found through the collective decision to make the tribunal organizing process a struggle against the isolation and criminalization of movements, and by extension, of political prisoners. To this end, international jurists from over twenty-seven countries listened to dozens of expert witnesses—activists, academics, family members, clergy, movement leaders—testify about their experiences of state repression.

The tribunals were anchored by volunteers from different movements with a history of organizing and defense of political prisoners. Prisoner defense campaigns, attorneys, and prisoners stood at the center of these tribunals: the first tribunal focused on political repression while the subsequent ones used the existence of political prisoners as one example of U.S. internal colonialism. Crucial leadership was also extended by national liberation movement organizations such as the American Indian Movement, New Afrikan Peoples Organization, Movimiento de Liberación Nacional Mexicano, and Movimiento de Liberación Nacional Puertorriqueño and by solidarity organizations such as the National Committee to Free Puerto Rican Political Prisoners and Prisoners of War, the Prairie Fire Organizing Committee, the May 19 Communist Organization, and the John Brown Anti-Klan Organizing Committee. The support of antiwar and Christian left organizations, ranging from the National Council of Churches to the War Resisters League, expanded the tribunals' base of support.

Each of the three tribunals built on the success of the previous one. Activist and historian Richard Kekuni Blaisdell testified at the San Francisco Tribunal in 1992, and the organization he led, the ProKanaka Maoli Sovereignty Working Group, then helped convene the Ka Ho'okolokolonui Kānaka Maoli Tribunal in 1993 to elevate the issue of Hawaiian sovereignty. The 1992 tribunal used the occasion of the Columbian quincentennial, and the 1993 effort marked the one hundredth anniversary of the overthrow of Hawai'i's Queen Lili'uokalani. The nine-day Hawai'i tribunal visited each of the islands taken between the United States' so-called annexation of Hawai'i on August 12, 1898, and the proclamation of Hawaiian statehood on August 21, 1959, to center an indigenous claim for sovereignty against the United States on an international stage.

The 1990–93 tribunals contributed to a heightened consciousness about U.S. political prisoners, both within the communities they came from and broader U.S. civil society. They helped to build the capacity and reach of their organizational members and to build toward gains such as the 1998 National Jericho March to Free All Political Prisoners, which gave birth to the ongoing Jericho Amnesty Movement. The tribunals were particularly meaningful for the Puerto Rican independence movement, which built on their work to achieve several gains, including the release of eleven Puerto Rican political prisoners in 1999, the ouster of the U.S. Navy from Vieques in 2003 (following another tribunal in 2001), freedom for Puerto Rican political prisoner Carlos Alberto Torres in 2010, and the 2017 commutation of the sentence of Oscar López Rivera, long considered the "Mandela of the Americas."

Luis Alejandro Molina is a long-time organizer of the Puerto Rican Independence movement, one of the leaders of the Puerto Rican Cultural Center, and an editor and media producer who is currently working on a documentary about Oscar López Rivera.

PART TWO:
ART, ACTIVISM & ARCHIVES

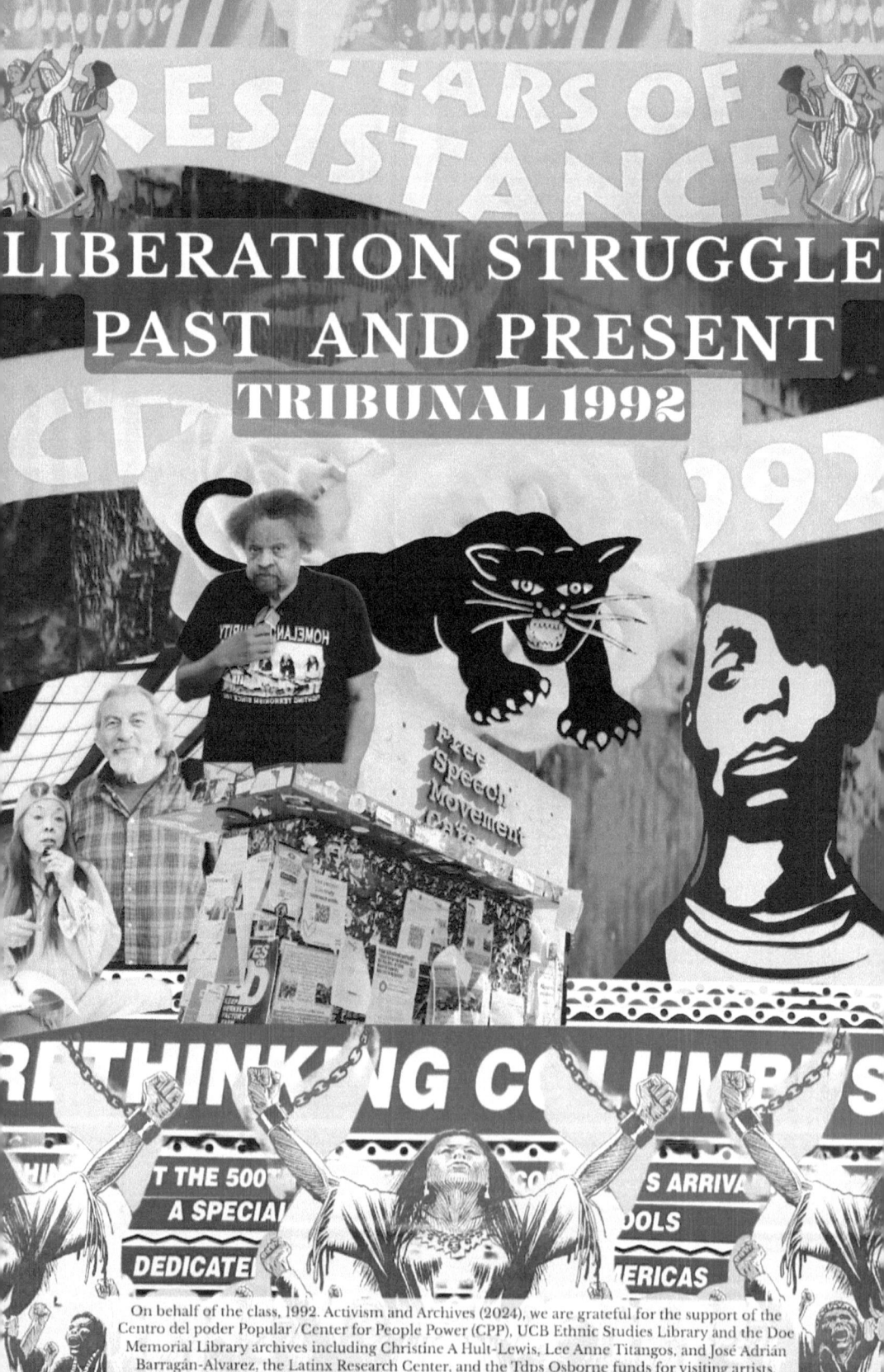

TEARS OF RESISTANCE

LIBERATION STRUGGLE
PAST AND PRESENT
TRIBUNAL 1992

On behalf of the class, 1992. Activism and Archives (2024), we are grateful for the support of the Centro del poder Popular / Center for People Power (CPP), UCB Ethnic Studies Library and the Doe Memorial Library archives including Christine A Hult-Lewis, Lee Anne Titangos, and José Adrián Barragán-Alvarez, the Latinx Research Center, and the Tdps Osborne funds for visiting artists.

1992: Liberation Struggles Past and Present

This catalog insert recuperates the active intergenerational resistance of the International Tribunal movement with reflection essays based on oral histories, artworks, and documents that are part of an exhibit presented at the Ethnic Studies Library in October 2025. The exhibit was planned alongside a discussion panel that took place the year prior as part of a course called 1992: Activism and the Archives[1] including the following speakers:

Arthur League

Arthur League was born in the American South, making his way as a young man to the City of Los Angeles, where he became an activist with the Southern California Chapter of the Black Panther Party in the protection of neighborhood residents against police brutality, poverty, and racist city management. His work in the Party, and as a speaker and organizer, continues to inspire truth and resilience for community self-determination. itsabouttimebpp.com

Claude Marks

Claude Marks is a journalist, scholar, researcher, and former political prisoner whose work as a media producer and analyst provides the insights of his life experience in liberation struggles. He is the founder and co-director of the Freedom Archives. Claude's work over the years in media, archives, documentary, and historiography makes it possible to safeguard the memories of social movements, making it one of the anchor institutions of our people. freedomarchives.org

Judith Talaugon

"Aunty" Judy Talaugon is a Chumash and Filipina Land Protector from the Santa Ynez Band of Chumash Indians. She is the lead organizer of the Tribunal Project. Growing up among Mexican and Filipina communities in California as the daughter of farmworkers and immigrant leaders, she is a lifetime activist in numerous struggles, ranging from human rights to housing, land back struggles, and the protection of water and land defenders. tribunalproject.org

---

1 The panel took place on October 17, 2024, organized by Seth Donnelly, as part of the course taught by Angela Marino. The class also visited and learned from archivists of the collections at Doe Memorial Library. Support for these events came from Prof. Marino, the D+M Lab, the Center for People Power, the Latinx Research Center, and the Shelly Osborne Guest Artist Fund of the Department of Theater, Dance, and Performance Studies. Art exhibit curators Nathaniel Moore worked with the support of the Ethnic Studies Library, partnered with the Freedom Archives, with assistance of Joaquin Min Antonio. Art collage as title page for Part 2 is by Lulu Matute with inspiration from images of Doe Memorial Library Archives. Art collage on the opposite page by Javier Mateos-Campos.

Panel Reflections

At the event held on October 17, 2024, in Wheeler Hall on the UC Berkeley campus, panelists Judith Talaugon, Arthur League, and Claude Marks discussed how a strong foundation and sense of community facilitate unity through recognized solidarity. I thought this was interesting and highly relevant, as we as a society today are extremely desensitized and let injustices fly over our heads. And when one is desensitized to one's own environment, then complacency allows unspeakable acts of oppression and violence to become the norm. The community building and strong sense of togetherness discussed among the panelists are what I find to be severely lacking in this day and age. Specifically, the spread of unreliable misinformation and the use of technology, particularly social media, are clouding the minds of the younger generation today. Social media is supposed to connect us, but it is quite evident that we have become isolated in our own echo chambers, destroying any sense of community that will also allow us to create change through recognized solidarity, fighting with Indigenous people, and all subjugated people of the U.S., as well as the world.

In the current socio-economic and political climate of the year 2025, the messages and themes that are propagated by these speakers are still extremely resonant and can be applied to the ever-changing world we are facing today, and the social movements that are born from it. In this era of misinformation and biased news organizations, heightened through the alienation and isolation that is a side-effect of the epidemic of social media, community building through a recognized solidarity has never been more crucial than it is now. There is a correlation between every single issue, whether that be Indigenous rights, racial justice, environmental issues, or economic fairness, showing that every struggle has a link stemming from an overarching history of colonial oppression that is still having repercussions on our society in the 21st century.

The panelists and these documents emphasized the critical importance of unification through collective sovereignty, a step in dismantling oppressive systems that have been in place for a millennium, which can only be achieved through recognition of said sovereignty.

Acknowledging these past wrongs together is only half the battle in navigating the issues we face today, as the real work of resistance begins with the strength of solid structures built upon the community's undying actions of unified people.

— Alexander Cole

What I see as most important from the 500 Years of Resistance activism to the present reality is that we must continue fighting. Sometimes, I am of the opinion that this battle for equality is pointless, that it will forever continue, never-ending, destined always to be fighting for something more. However, there are also times when it is important to keep the memory of those who have already fought for what we have, ensuring their sacrifice is not in vain. There are so many historical figures whom we make a point to remember, but what about those who have given their lives fighting against the struggle just to be left out of history? That is who we should be dedicating our struggle for: the people, who, without expecting more, decided that they wanted to fight for something greater than themselves. Something like this takes courage and grit; many people today like to believe they have.

This leads me to another critical point in the context of the 500 Years of Resistance: the choice to fight against struggle is a continuous one, not a one-and-done deal. All three of our panelists had already lived a life full of conflict, despair, and victory. That was the lesson I derived from our panelists: fighting against powers determined to put the rest of us down is a lifelong endeavor. I have always been afraid to speak up because I am afraid of becoming a political prisoner like many of our panelists. However, that in itself is something for everyone to be angry about, the idea that some of us can be afraid of speaking out because we feel as though our government will punish us. That's exactly why I feel so inspired by our panelists; despite all the adversity they faced, they are still able to sit in front of us and tell us to continue fighting.

— Brandon Cruz

Dangerous Memories

Invasion and Resistance
Since 1492

Remember us after we are gone. Don't forget us. Conjure up our faces and our words. Our image will be as a tear in the hearts of those who want to remember us.

Popol Vuh - Sacred Mayan Book

A Publication of the Chicago Religious Task Force on Central America

Dangerous Memories: Invasion and Resistance Since 1492
Chicago Religious Task Force on Central America
1991
Book Cover

Dangerous Memories

Abby Román

The image of Dangerous Memories that stands before you is more than just a depiction of history; it is a visual testament to survival, resistance, and the ongoing fight for justice. It serves as a reminder of the Spanish invasion of the Western Hemisphere and the immense suffering it unleashed on Indigenous peoples and other oppressed communities. This piece is an emblem of light in a dark tunnel that only pushes forward, asking us to question the sanitized narratives that we have been fed, and instead recognize the truth of Indigenous peoples' experiences.

European colonizers understood that controlling memory was key to controlling people. The European conquistadors who arrived in Abya Yala (the Americas) sought not only to seize land but to erase Indigenous identities, languages, and ways of knowing. Forced assimilation—through boarding schools, religious conversion, and the criminalization of Indigenous practices—was a deliberate strategy to sever Indigenous peoples from their histories and communities.

Memories become dangerous to the oppressor because they are a reminder that they cannot and will not suppress them. This is why colonizers sought to erase Indigenous histories, languages, and ways of knowing—because remembering is an act of resistance. The European conquistadors who arrived in the Western Hemisphere understood the power of obliterating memories. The image serves as a reminder of the Spanish invasion and the suffering it unleashed, as it strives to expose the true nature of the events of 1492—not as a discovery of a new land, but as the destruction and disassembling of it.

Images have the power to unsettle, disrupt, and force a confrontation with the truth. Dangerous Memories—a spear piercing a back, a horrified woman frozen in terror— demands recognition to heal the violence that has shaped history and continues to reverberate today. The depiction of a spear through the back symbolizes the treachery of colonial conquest. It reflects the brutal tactics used by European invaders who arrived under the mask of peace but brought obliteration. This imagery reflects the broken treaties, the deception, and the slaughter that Indigenous nations faced. It forces viewers to acknowledge the historical truth that colonization was not an accident, but a deliberate act of subjugation.

The woman's expression of horror captures the raw emotional toll of colonial violence. She represents Indigenous women who witnessed the destruction of their families, their lands, and their ways of life. Her presence in the image serves as a reminder that conquest was not only a military invasion but a deeply personal and generational trauma. It speaks to the violence against Indigenous women, the forced removals, and the attempted erasure of culture. Art, when it presents disturbing imagery, becomes a tool for education and activism. This image functions as a visual narrative of resilience, ensuring that the true stories of Indigenous peoples are neither forgotten nor misrepresented.

Indigenous stories are vital, and Dangerous Memories serves as a visual narrative of resilience and survival for Indigenous communities. It holds the collective voices of many, capturing the reality of experience and the enduring impact of colonization. Each detail speaks to the truths that Indigenous peoples have lived and the strength required to sustain their cultures and histories in the face of relentless adversity. It's more than a picture—it's a living testament to their stories, their rights, and the ongoing fight for justice and self-determination.

Let the hope of this piece, of your dangerous memories, seep into your actions. Let these memories guide you toward truth, toward resistance, and toward a future where justice prevails.

"...If you want to know what we are who become animate at the rain's metallic ring, the stone's accumulated strength, who tremble in the wind's blossoming (that enervates earth's potentialities), who stir just as flowers unfold to the sun;..."

If you want to know what we are
WE ARE REVOLUTION!

—by Carlos Bulosan[1]

1 Excerpt from *If You Want to Know What We Are: A Carlos Bulosan Reader*. Ed. E. San Juan, Jr. Minneapolis: West End Press, 1983.

Diss'ing the "Discovery"

columbus design by Elspeth Meyer

Political Prisoners and Prisoners of War in U.S. Prisons

De-Celebrate

the Columbus Quincentennary

and affirm

500 Years Of Resistance

❀

with contributions from

* Sundiata Acoli * Marilyn Buck * Mark Cook * Edwin Cortés *

* Elizam Escobar * Larry Giddings * David Gilbert *

* Jaan Laaman * Mondo Langa * Ray Levasseur * Alberto Rodríguez *

and updates on

* Mumia Abu-Jamal * Norma Jean Croy * Leonard Peltier *

Diss'ing the "Discovery"
Political Prisoners and Prisoners of War in U.S. Prisons De-Celebrate the
Columbus Quincentenary and affirm 500 Years of Resistance
Cover Design Elspeth Meyer
1992
Monograph

Diss'ing the "Discovery" is a political booklet centered on critiquing the legacy of Christopher Columbus and the impact of colonialism, with a focus on U.S. imperialism, racism, and resistance movements. It was created in 1992 by political activists and U.S. political prisoners, Sundiata Acoli, Marilyn Buck, Larry Giddings, David Gilbert, Jaan Laaman, Ray Levasseur, Mark Cook, Mondo Langa, Edwin Cortés, Elizam Escobar, and Alberto Rodríguez including co-editors Meg Starr and Barbara Zeller to counter such celebrations, presenting Columbus not as a hero, but as a symbol of genocide, imperialism, and ongoing oppression.

The purpose of this collection of essays, images, letters, poems, and analysis is to document acts of resistance and to inspire continued solidarity with oppressed peoples across the Americas. It features contributions from political prisoners and prisoners of war, providing firsthand commentary in personal reflections. The layout is purposeful yet straightforward, reflecting the grassroots nature of the publication, including a wanted poster of Christopher Columbus for his crimes against humanity (Gilbert 5), a circle design message that says, "Free Norma Jean Croy" (The Norma Jean Croy Defense Committee 13), followed by another poster saying, "Save Mumia Abu-Jamal!" (Mumia Abu Jamal Faces Imminent Execution 17). These stories become the shadow of history, stories that need a light on them so they can be told.

The booklet was made in solidarity for those who have been negatively impacted by Columbus's arrival and whose stories needed to be heard. It was made to de-glorify Columbus to emphasize what Michel Rolph-Trouillot called the importance of the completed story (Trouillot 3). The document is a compilation, which alone is a demonstration of various people trying to preserve their own story and culture. Trouillot's Epilogue, "Good Day, Columbus," is about how Columbus Day is a celebration of selective history, "Madrid's promotion of Columbus as the day of Hispanity…" (134). Trouillot is exploring the variation in the way Columbus is portrayed, often to sugarcoat what he truly did. This further shows how, from the 500 years of resistance to the present reality, we are not necessarily trying to rewrite history; instead, we are constantly trying to correct it. To correct history, we need to preserve the diverse cultures and personal stories, so we can move beyond the narrative told from the perspective of those in power.

I personally believe that telling stories helps prolong their legacy and impact on the world. This is because the impact that these stories leave on me helps me create a wider perspective on the world. A strong continuity that holds is the urge for a complete perspective on history shown in these documents, readings, and oral histories. There are so many stories being told that we need to constantly synthesize and change our perspective to understand them.

— Juna Park

The politically explosive booklet Diss'ing the 'Discovery' was produced in response to the 500th anniversary of Columbus's invasion of the Americas. Bold, all-caps lettering runs across the cover calling for the release of political prisoners, decolonization, and resistance. "De-Celebrate the Columbus Quincentenary," and "500 Years of Resistance," among other opening lines, emphasize the book's opposition to the narrative that celebrates Columbus's arrival. With essays, poems, private letters, and artworks supplied by activists and prisoners, the layout is jam-packed with text inside, boosting voices of solidarity and resistance. The contributors' prominent listing on the cover highlights their importance as political prisoners or activists whose stories serve as the foundation for the publication's themes.

Reflecting on the panel discussion, I found that each activist's story conveyed a powerful blend of personal experience and collective resistance, demonstrating how individual journeys shape the fabric of a social movement. The activists' accounts highlighted a deep commitment to addressing structural injustices, showing not only resilience but also adaptability in the face of change. They stressed the importance of solidarity within their communities and the role of shared experiences in sustaining morale and purpose. This social aspect, a crucial foundation in movements, cultivates a sense of belonging and mutual support, motivating members to continue despite the obstacles they face. Their commitment reminded me of how community shapes resistance, creating a space where individuals find strength in shared struggles and build collective action as an ongoing form of resistance.

In examining this within the framework of performance art pieces like Couple in the Cage, I noticed a parallel in how activists use performative actions to resist and raise awareness. Just as the performance art piece subverts perceptions of discovery and colonialism, the activists' narratives challenge conventional views of power and societal roles. These stories, rich with real experiences and emotion, serve as powerful testimony, directly challenging dominant narratives and exposing deeper truths about the systems they resist. The discussion reinforced that these movements are not merely reactive; they are proactive in constructing new understandings and redefining social norms. This interpretive framework illuminates the nuanced ways that activism can echo performance art, using lived experiences to inform, disrupt, and redefine the collective narrative of resistance.

What stands out most from Diss'ing the "Discovery" and the themes it explores of 500 Years of Resistance is the persistence of Indigenous, Black, and other marginalized groups to demand recognition, justice, and self-determination despite enduring systemic violence and oppression. The document underscores how historical patterns of resistance have been crucial in uniting these communities against forces of imperialism and exploitation, emphasizing that this resistance is not merely a series of events in the past but a continuous struggle that evolves and adapts. From Columbus's arrival, which initiated a violent transformation of entire societies, to the modern-day activism around political prisoners, this material highlights how historical events remain deeply embedded in today's structures of power and inequity. The voices within the booklet represent both personal and collective resilience, speaking to the necessity of remembering these histories to fuel contemporary movements.

As someone living more than 30 years later, it's clear that this document resonates with present-day social justice movements, from the ongoing fight for Indigenous sovereignty to the demands to end mass incarceration. What I see as most relevant is how this historical narrative helps bridge past injustices with today's calls for systemic change, showing us how understanding these legacies can empower new generations of activists. Today, movements like Black Lives Matter, Indigenous land rights advocacy, and the push to dismantle oppressive systems like prisons and borders mirror the resistance outlined in this document. The voices from "Diss'ing the Discovery" push us to interpret history not as a closed chapter but as an ongoing narrative that demands our participation, urging us to both acknowledge the weight of the past and confront the pressing need for justice in the present. This material shows that true change involves challenging established narratives and that today's activism is part of a broader, centuries-long struggle for a world defined by equity and respect for all people.

— Mingshu Ci

500 Years of Resistance: Sonoma County Free Press
Cover Art Tom Yeates
1992
Periodical

SEPTEMBER ISSUE Vol. 6 No.4 1992

500 YEARS of RESISTANCE

A SPECIAL ISSUE OF THE
SONOMA COUNTY
FREE PRESS

P.O. Box 863
Occidental, Ca. 95465

Bulk Rate-U.S. Postage Paid
Permit No. 7, Occidental, Ca. 95465

THANK YOU FOR SUBSCRIBING

57

500 Years of Resistance
1492-1992

The Quincentennial celebration of Columbus' "discovery" of the Americas marks an important time in our history—a turning point. It is time to dispel the lingering myths and shatter the legacy of Columbus that still exists today.

Indigenous peoples and other peoples of color throughout the Americas suffer still from the pervasive notions of manifest destiny, ownership of land and greed. It is those same peoples who resist and fight those notions today, just as they have fought for the last 500 years.

On October 12, 1992, the eyes of the world will be on the Americas, particularly the U.S. Many will celebrate the 500th anniversay of this "discovery". Most of the world, however, will remember the last 500 years as a fight against genocide, racism, colonialism and political internment.

All across the U.S. and the world, people are resisting the governments call for a celebration and are remembering this year to be a year of International Solidarity with Indigenous People. As well as a year to fight for self-determination of oppressed nationalities within U.S. borders and to demand the release of all Political Prisoners and Prisoners of War.

The National Freedom Now Networks have 5 Basic Points of Unity:

1. Recognition of the sovereign rights of the Indigenous Peoples in the Americas;
   - a.) Recognition of the transnational character and struggles of the Indigenous Peoples in the Americas that transcend artificial geo-political boundries;
   - b) Recognition of the League of Indigenous Soverign Indian nations and the International Indian Treaty Council to assume its rightful seat in the UN General Assembly and other appropriate UN bodies.

2. Abolition and dismemberment of the US federal state and all other white supremacist empires and states in the Americas;
   - a) Recognition of the New Afrikan nation and its struggles to establish an independent New Afrikan State;
   - b) Recognition of Northern Mexico as a legitimate part of the Mexican nation and support of the struggle for the liberation and socialist reunification of Mexico;
   - c) Support for the independence of Puerto Rico;
   - d) Consultation and discussion between the Indigenous Peoples' and the oppressed nations within the US colonial empire toward developing treaties which support and guarentee self-determination and independence for all oppressed nations in the US.

3. Development of a democratic, socialist confederation of all liberated nations in the US.

4. Freedom for All Political Prisoners & Prisoners of War in North America.

5. Support of all freedom-loving and justice minded people for the above.

Freedom Now National Networks

500 Years of Resistance: 1492-1992
Freedom Now Network
1992
Pamphlet / Insert

With the inspiring voices of the panelists who spoke with our class in mind, I began reading and analyzing the work of 500 Years of Resistance. I realized that the language in the document was not unique to this individual cause, but it was grounded and intentional, similar to the words spoken by *all* of our panelists. It was immediately clear to me that this text and these panelists were connected in that they represent and result from each unique demographic's lived experiences and devastating realities. The most important takeaway from this connection is that raising awareness only goes so far, if not paired with concrete action – they must go *hand in hand* to be truly beneficial.

In our modern technological age, raising awareness and discussing social and political justice has become part of our everyday lives. While it's good to raise awareness, a disappearing Instagram story only creates a false sense of accomplishment. It is not enough to make a change, not enough to stir strong feelings of resistance in the general public. It's become such a commonplace "action" to acknowledge how sad or upsetting something might be that the general public has become desensitized to these real-world problems, and all of the hard work falls on the handful of people who fight for said cause. I believe this modern predicament of humanity to be a side effect of the overstimulating, fast-paced information-dumping we subject our minds to daily through our devices. There's a severe dichotomy between reading news of inhumane practices a few times a week in the paper and being bombarded with flashy articles, posts, reels, and images on every social media platform multiple times a day. Perhaps a couple of decades ago, the same devastating news would have had a much more shocking effect on the general public. Still, today, we have succinct conversations to raise awareness and perhaps inspire one or two people to take action.

This difference is evident in the text – while the first page is a call to action with statements of the Freedom Now Network's intentions, the rest of the brochure informs readers of various meetings and resources to encourage involvement in the activism. The first page contextualizes the purpose of the program, explaining that some people will be celebrating the 500th anniversary of Columbus's discovery, but most of the world will be remembering the 500 years of fighting "against genocide, racism, colonialism, and political internment" (1). Next, a 3-month calendar of events is included, with April's content being centered around Puerto Rican Prisoners of War and Indigenous Political Prisoners, May's events shifting into awareness about the prison system and women, and June's lineup focusing on more generalized "problems of America" with AIDs, Malcolm X, racism, class, indigenous rights, political prisoners, and POWs. Finally, the last page has a section that informs readers where their organization has centers for information and an advertisement for a book about political prisoners in the U.S. The last page serves as a demonstration of encouraging people to adopt more active political and social mindsets.

While Instagram infographics often include suggestions for "next steps," they primarily serve as conceptual containers for brainstormed ideas, aiming to raise awareness rather than drive action. Many of the references we studied in class included ways to learn more, but activists were conscious of the prerogative to take action. The panelists are living, breathing examples of active change, and their experiences influenced my desire to observe the diachronic change in how activism is carried out. Their passion, dedication, and tireless work led to the protection and historical memory of the I-Hotel, the truthful coverage of protests here at Cal, and the efforts to return stolen Indigenous lands.

—Sarine Danielle Baronian

The layout of the 500 Years of Resistance document is similar to a manifesto, advocating for Indigenous rights and the abolition of colonial systems in the Americas. It's built around five key points, each advocating for Indigenous self-determination, unity, and support for other oppressed groups. The language is clear and direct, showing a strong push for change and resistance against existing colonial structures. For instance, one point calls for the "abolition and dismemberment of the U.S. federal state and all other white supremacist empires and states in the Americas," which reflects the document's bold approach to challenging current systems and envisioning a liberated future. Each point includes specific goals, like gaining recognition for Indigenous groups in the United Nations and supporting Puerto Rican independence. The structure, with each section focusing on different areas of freedom and resistance, reinforces the document's call for a unified front against colonial oppression.

This message of Indigenous empowerment and resistance ties in with the idea that colonial powers often control which histories are recorded and passed down. In *The Archive and the Repertoire*, Diana Taylor talks about how archives have historically erased Indigenous voices by prioritizing written records over lived experiences, a pattern that keeps colonial viewpoints dominant (Taylor, pp. 28). Rather than accepting historical erasure, the document calls for concrete changes and invites Indigenous communities to assert their histories and identities in ways that resist colonial narratives, aligning with Taylor's ideas about the importance of preserving non-colonial histories.

Looking more closely at 500 Years of Resistance, it's clear that the document focuses not just on political independence but also on reclaiming and celebrating Indigenous culture and identity. It strongly opposes any efforts to make Indigenous people fit into colonial molds, pushing instead for the preservation of unique languages, traditions, and values as ways to resist cultural erasure. The manifesto argues that true freedom isn't just about land or governance, it's also about protecting Indigenous ways of life from being overwritten by colonial narratives. One of its core messages is the need for an education system that honors Indigenous histories and knowledge, rather than one shaped by colonial values that attempt to erase or "correct" them. By focusing on cultural pride and self-determination, 500 Years of Resistance aims to inspire future generations to stay connected to their roots, building a strong foundation for Indigenous identity that stands apart from colonial influence. This emphasis on cultural strength and resilience connects closely with what Jessica Horton describes in James Luna's art, where he challenges colonial stereotypes and uses performance to celebrate Indigenous identity and history (Horton, p. 63). Both the manifesto and Luna's work contribute to a larger movement to reclaim Indigenous stories and keep these traditions alive in the face of ongoing challenges.

Reflecting specifically on panelists Judy and Arthur, their stories from in-class as well as their stories published online gave me a close-up look at what it means to be an activist fighting for Indigenous and Black communities. Judy talks about growing up with the constant pressure to fit in, to blend in with mainstream society, and even to identify as Mexican to avoid discrimination. For her, this struggle is deeply connected to her family's history and the lasting impact of colonialism. She shares how her father's experience of abandonment and hardship influenced her own journey, creating a "legacy" of resilience in the face of erasure. Judy is passionate about passing down origin stories, traditional practices, and knowledge to the next generation. She describes this as essential work—not just to keep traditions alive, but to help young people feel proud of who they are. Teaching her students about Indigenous heritage and culture isn't just education for Judy; it's an act of defiance, a way to make sure that Indigenous identities continue to thrive despite centuries of efforts to erase them. This dedication ties directly into the message of 500 Years of Resistance, which calls for protecting and reclaiming Indigenous stories and histories as an act of cultural survival.

Arthur's experiences with the Black Panther Party highlight another side of resistance, one focused on community defense and empowerment against police violence. He recalls moving from Tennessee to Los Angeles and being shocked by the level of police brutality, which was even more intense than what he'd seen in the South. League describes how the Black Panther Party took a hands-on approach to protecting Black communities—they'd stand watch with guns in their neighborhoods, making sure people knew their rights and were safe from police harassment. Although he noted how this wasn't just about self-defense, the Panthers also worked to uplift their community by setting up breakfast programs for kids and providing educational resources. Arthur explains how this sense of unity and collective care was central to the Panthers' mission. To him, it was about building a real community, where people had each other's backs and worked together to survive and resist. Both Judy and League's stories bring out the real-life struggles and sacrifices behind 500 Years of Resistance's call for unity and self-determination. They show how, for both Indigenous and Black communities, resisting oppression means fighting not only for survival but also for the preservation of identity and culture.

The 500 Years of Resistance document connects deeply with today's struggles for justice, especially around reclaiming identity, culture, and land. One of the biggest takeaways from the document is how it emphasizes these actions as core parts of resistance, not just responses to oppression. This feels incredibly relevant in 2025, as we see movements that increase awareness of the environmental impacts on Indigenous lands. Even in Berkeley, there is always an acknowledgement during events of the Indigenous land we are on. The manifesto's call for solidarity among oppressed groups reminds us that many of today's issues are connected: racial justice, environmental activism, and Indigenous rights. Judy and Arthur both talked about how holding onto culture, community, and stories has been a way to survive and resist, which is something we see today as people work to reclaim spaces and practices that colonialism tried to erase.

Thinking about 500 Years of Resistance alongside the experiences shared by the panelists gives us a way to understand today's activism through a wider historical lens. Judy's dedication to preserving Indigenous heritage, Arthur's memories of the Black Panther Party's community defense, and Claude's reflection on being an anti-war activist show that today's movements are part of a much longer story of resistance. It's a reminder that the work people are doing now isn't new, that it's part of a generational fight for justice. This fight for justice I see in the panelists is something I see in myself and my peers as well. Change is an ongoing commitment to protecting identity, community, and autonomy. This perspective is empowering because it shows that the values, stories, and knowledge of marginalized communities have survived through centuries of erasure and continue to inspire people. 500 Years of Resistance reminds us that today's movements are about building a future that respects these histories and keeps them alive, not just reacting to problems as they pop up.

—Keira Duong Lam

"Remerica," a word created by the great African-American playwright, poet and activist, Amiri Baraka, mirrors the many feelings, attitudes and historical events ingrained in the memory and oral tradition of the oppressed. Remerica is an old, basic form of information trasferrally passed from generation to generation, questioning and challenging the history written by the colonists. Remerica is the cross-examination and deconstruction of an invented and inaccurate past to bring to light the concepts of truth, love, equality, justice, and humanity. Remerica is about America, an antithesis of Amerika.' Amerika, with the letter k, points to the fact that among many problems contrary to the 'American Dream,' the United States can tolerate a Ku Klux Klansman running for governor of a state and campaigning for president of the United States, and consider this normal and 'democratic.'

It is in this spirit that the artists in Remerica ! Amerika express in their art the positive values of our heritage in reasserting our cultural and historical integrity and roots. This same spirit has awakened us fom the genocidal slow sleep of death imported by the three caravelas/skulls of Cristoforo Columbo, and we now rejoice in life as we shift towards the light of hope."[1]

—Juan Sánchez

Remerica ! Amerika
1492   1992
Sept 8-Oct 30, 1992, Hunter College

Organized and with essay by Juan Sánchez;
Curitorial assistance and additional essays
by Enoc Perez and Miguelangel Ruiz;
invited contributors Coco Fusco and Guillermo Gómez-Peña.

1 This excerpt appeared in the catalog for the Hunter College exhibit Remerica Amerika with the credits listed above.

Remerica – Amerika
Juan Sánchez
9/8/1992
Catalog

The document Remerica - Amerika is the catalog for an exhibit containing about 40 pages of images of artwork and essays, including poetry, photography, newspapers, drawings, collages, posters, sculptures, and paintings, included in an exhibit by the same name. The exhibition, presented in 1992 at Hunter College in New York City, curated by Juan Sánchez, marked the 500th year of the genocide of Indigenous people in the Americas. One piece of artwork I would like to discuss is by Rupert García. García shares a drawing where we see the outline of Christopher Columbus, behind which is a distressed skeleton (Sánchez). What I believe this artwork is trying to show is that Columbus is the forefront of the death of millions.

For centuries, we were told to celebrate Christopher Columbus. Those in power have at times failed to acknowledge history and the effects of past events that remain today. At present, those in power are refusing to acknowledge what is happening around the world. Examining the catalog for Remerica-Amerika is impactful, revealing it not only as an archive but also as a space to showcase and highlight history. It's important to avoid becoming numb to what happened in history and what is happening in the present. It is important not to lose our empathy. It is essential to create spaces to allow those to share their experiences.

Being in a space where I was able to hear from activists like Arthur League, Judy Talaugon, and Claude Marks was very inspiring and eye-opening. It was interesting to hear how many started their journey as activists when they were young, for example, in college. I enjoyed hearing the passion they have and the knowledge they shared with us. It was inspiring to see how the activists also supported one another and their cause. It just shows how working together is also a form of resistance.

Hearing League's story, his time in Los Angeles, and his involvement with the Black Panther chapter in Los Angeles were the most memorable parts for me, as I hadn't heard much about the history of the Black Panthers in Los Angeles. I'm from Los Angeles, so I appreciated hearing about one's experience in the city and how they contributed to helping the city. Also, it resonated with me when League discussed the women who inspire him because I feel inspired by the women in my life as well.

After reviewing the document and hearing from activists, I find that the most crucial takeaway from 500 years of resistance to the present is that the fight is not over. Many still use the term "post-colonial," yet in reality, we are still living through colonization. It is crucial to acknowledge the history of the past by doing research, hearing, and engaging with the stories of those who lived through it. Having the opportunity to listen to the stories of those who lived through critical times in our history was impactful. Hearing stories from personal experiences helps us build empathy.

In 2024, we are still seeing colonization and imperialism happening around us. We are still seeing forms of resistance, like groups around the world advocating to stop the genocide in Palestine. We are still seeing politicians siding against us, on the side of greed. We are still seeing how those in power try to gaslight the world into believing colonization and genocide are not happening.

—Delmi Belloso

From the very first page, Remerica - Amerika is starkly and artistically woven with subtextual intent and meaning. It's in black and white. In color, some of the images could be beautiful, but the plainness has a cut to it: a cascading collage of upside-down portraits of Columbus, juxtaposed words under 'Pax Americana Quintessential' split between black and white, and many more images, drawings, essays, and words. All the elements of the tribunal feel interconnected, presumably thematically, but also in a stylistic sense as if there is a continuing train of thought with the line between separate art forms blended under this continuing thread.

In the Acknowledgements Susan H. Edwards writes, "We are indebted to Professor Sánchez for bringing to our gallery the visual voices of a diverse group of artists from the African American, Asian-American, Latin-American, and Native-American communities. With this exhibition, we hope to validate the words of Barbara Jordan, who said, 'We honor cultural identity. America's strength is rooted in its diversity.' Professor Sánchez invited each artist to create an original work of art to be exhibited in the Bertha and Karl Leubsdorf Art Gallery at Hunter College and another work specifically for the artists' book, which accompanies the exhibition." In Sánchez's own words in an essay written at the beginning of the tribunal, "In spite of 500 years of genocide and physical conquest, spiritual conquest never took place." I think this perfectly encapsulates the motivation behind Remerica - Amerika: to push on the spiritual front, of which there is an undying hope, where the existence of an idea among people is power in and of itself.

The same sentiment was reflected by the panel activists who came to visit on October 17th. Perspective is so important, and the world changes dramatically when you don't know that it will or even can change. It's hard to imagine Berkeley in an actual war-like riot, with tear gas and explicit intervention, and yet, there are many people still alive who have experienced it. It's these personal experiences that make theory real, that show the qualities of the realization of dreams, and how nonlinear things can often be. Some things may take less time, and others more; there are so many gray lines and uncertainties that the idea of truth seems to be increasingly cemented in me as a life compass. We move in directions towards what we believe in to the best of our ability, and in the end, that's all we can really do. Something as intense as activism especially requires and intertwines everything in life. There's so much that matters, so much to relish, so much beauty if you look for it, and it's that dynamic between both pushing for change and momentum while not forgetting the details where purpose lies. It's a mode of listening, acting, and embracing.

Remerica - Amerika has a grim solemnity that plays with a contention for change—it does not make it a spectacle, but envisions it. It carries the grounded oddity of change, the perspective, scale, and pines at a deep point. There is an excerpt by Papo Colo from the Hybrid State Manifesto, 1982-1992, over an image of two kids looking out of a cage-like structure. The cage structure itself has a phantom quality to it: it's difficult to see its dimensions, almost resembling a net, as if it's hard to see what is boxing them in to begin with.

"The Hybrid State is the union and reunion of dilapidated static cultures into the centrifugal force of building and rebuilding a dynamic nation, of shaping and reshaping a new culture from the assemblage of cultures into the language of multiple options of choice, into a general vision of our sensibilities. The phenomena of the Hybrid State make you a participant in and witness to other cultures, without losing your own." This idea brings to mind the word 'Remerica,' a remake into something cumulative yet non-smothering. The focus is not solely on the past 500 years of colonialism, its a view of the future.

Personally, it is this view of the future that I find most compelling. To begin to develop a way forward, you must not only identify what needs to change, but also what shouldn't. In other words, it can be easy to see your ideals. Still, you must also consider different perspectives that may contradict your thoughts, and the methodology for communicating and actualizing such a thing evolves with increasing nuance. Yet at the same time, it's not a matter of being 'realistic.' You shouldn't handicap or censor yourself based on what you believe to be possible, but it's an evolution.

Everything is cause-and-effect; nothing exists in isolation. We learn from what things are to see what they could become, and we extrapolate from what they were to see the processes of change. We must be open to the present and any signs of error while pushing forward to the best of our abilities. It is from the 500 years that we see that cultures need not only to be re-empowered, but reintegrated, as the very concept of culture is malleable and constantly changing.

We are all just people living on this planet, and the only way to move beyond a cycle of violence is to find that common ground. In a similar thread, I think it's important to note that everything happens for a reason, too: some factors lead to events, and the effects are all in a flow. Perhaps Remerica - Amerika is about the nature of change, real lasting change, in reaction to 500 years of persisting issues. There is a humble longing in the art that is as speculative as it is intentional. It's learning as it goes. After all, in the end, we don't know much, yet we do the best we can in the time we have.

—Theodore Dupont

VERDICT

OF THE INTERNATIONAL TRIBUNAL OF INDIGENOUS PEOPLES AND OPPRESSED NATIONS IN THE USA

Verdict of the International Tribunal of Indigenous
Peoples and Oppressed Nations in the USA
Oct 4, 1992
Monograph

The Verdict

The Verdict is a document that records the verdict of the International
Tribunal of Indigenous Peoples and Oppressed Nations in the USA. It lists the
37 primary reasons why the government is brought to court, divided into
three different parts. The first section points out the main goal: "That everyone resists, that no one stays behind." It also introduces the background of
this event and the reasons why witnesses brought the U.S. government to
court. In the second section, the document discusses the crimes committed
by the U.S. federal government and the laws it broke. Right after, it lists the
bill of particulars against the Federal Government. Different groups form the
prosecution team: The Native American Peoples, the New Afrikan People,
the Mexicano People, the People and State of Puerto Rico, and the International Criminal Conspiracy and Criminal Organization. People from diverse
backgrounds formed a large community that brought the United States to
court. The last but not least section of the paper discusses the laws that the
U.S. federal government, as identified by the court ruling, was found to have
broken.

From the second page, we can see that distinguished jurors comprising
the international tribunal and distinguished witnesses appearing before the
international tribunal are all part of the participants in this event. It's interesting that the publication information also includes information on how we
can call the American Indian Movement to obtain a copy of this verdict. From
that page, I also learned that seven people who come from different backgrounds and cultures collaborated to create this document. Interestingly, I
found that one of the seven jurors is from UC Berkeley!

Aside from learning about the role of archives and activists, we can also
learn the close connection between history and social movements. The activists Judy Talaugon and Claude Marks pointed to the Chinese Exclusion Act,
as well as Racial Segregation and Discrimination that happened during the
I-Hotel and Red Guard. After hearing Judy Talaugon's story as an activist, I

understand that no matter how difficult the situation is, there will always be some activists who stand up bravely. During the Red Guard talk by Claude Marks, he discussed how a group of primarily young Asian American activists, including many students and recent graduates, broke through the shackles on Asian Americans to start the movement. The event draws inspiration from the Black Panther Party and from the Red Guard movements in China.

Geography does not limit the thoughts and movements: people from different backgrounds and cultures can all come together, moving toward the same goal. After learning about archives and hearing the stories of movement activists, I came to realize the importance of understanding how history brings us together and leads us to where we are today. History is not simply linear; it spirals. We find that it continues to reveal recurring issues like colonization. Therefore, we need to learn from what happened back then, take from those movements, and move forward. As a member of the community myself, I feel a sense of responsibility that awakens within me. I should also put my efforts into this ongoing process of fighting for rights and equality. Also, it is essential to acknowledge what we have gotten from the movements and the sacrifices of those who came before us. Now, after learning this lesson, I will stand up for my community, using theater and art as a tool to bring public attention to events happening around the world.

During my research on the I-Hotel and the Red Guard movement, I was amazed to find that most of the activists involved were around the same age as me. The young generation holds the power to make change. Although the environment is not the same as it was back in the 1990s, the core ideas of equity, freedom, and human rights remain constant. I frequently watch as students hold speeches and parades on campus about issues they care about, from daily life issues to conflicts around the world. As a college student myself, I am inspired and feel I am also related to present-day movements for change. As the new power of society, we should think outside the box, keep our eyes open, and stand up for injustice and unfair power to fight for our community.

—Jingyi Zhou

The document, entitled 1992 Tribunal Verdict, is a formal report orga-nized with an introduction, specific charges, and verdicts, making the content accessible and also clarifying terms such as "crimes against humanity," "co-lonialism," and "genocide." The language is direct and often legalistic, under-scoring the document's aim to present an official legal indictment. It accuses the United States government of systematic oppression against Indigenous and marginalized populations, and seeks justice for these wrongdoings.

The International Tribunal was created in 1992 by a coalition of activists from a diverse background of anti-colonial, Indigenous, and human rights movements, aiming to address and expose the impacts of 500 years of colo-nialism. This was the 500th anniversary of Columbus's landing in the Carib-bean, which U.S. officials celebrated despite the onslaught of genocide that ensued. By creating this document, these activists sought to highlight the on-going injustices and demand historical accountability from powerful Western nations. The tribunal functioned as a means for people directly affected by colonialism to share their stories, name systemic wrongs, and demand repar-ative justice. The document stands as both a record of historical wrongs and a call to action, bringing these issues to light in hopes of catalyzing awareness and change.

The October 17th panel discussion with movement activists added a deeply personal perspective to understanding this document. The activists shared stories of their lived experiences within contemporary resistance movements, illustrating the social and human impacts of resistance work. They highlighted the personal and collective challenges that activists face— ranging from surveillance and social stigma to the physical and emotional toll of constant resistance. One activist spoke about the importance of sto-rytelling as a form of power, which is mirrored in the tribunal document's focus on testimony as a foundational part of the document. Another panelist discussed the idea of "intergenerational solidarity," emphasizing how today's movements build on the past, drawing direct lines from historical struggles to modern forms of resistance. Their stories provided a framework for in-terpreting the tribunal document not only as a formal accusation but as an active part of a lived social history of resistance.

The panelists also noted how performance art can serve as a vehicle for activism, breaking down complex social issues in ways that reach and resonate with audiences. The performance art pieces reviewed in class highlighted this point vividly, using body language, silence, and movement to convey stories that words often cannot. One piece, for example, explored themes of erasure and invisibility by having the performer gradually disappear into a background of colonial symbols. Such performances are critical to the resistance narrative, offering ways to confront the trauma of colonialism and reclaim personal and cultural agency. This is similar to how the Tribunal document is structured around storytelling, as both rely on bearing witness to the past and affirming identity through expression. These insights from the panelists underscore the importance of cultural and artistic forms of resistance, both in historic documents like the tribunal and in contemporary movements.

Reflecting on the past 500 years of resistance to colonialism concerning today's realities reveals that many of the core struggles remain ongoing. The Tribunal document underscores a need for accountability and acknowledgment of harm, and that theme echoes through today's movements. The activists from the panel reinforced that colonial violence, while transformed, is still present in various systems—economic inequality, racial discrimination, and environmental degradation. What stands out as most important from both the document and the contemporary discussion is that the act of resistance is an assertion of existence and survival. This assertion takes shape in many forms, whether through direct protest, storytelling, art, or legal documents like the Tribunal report, all creating a continuum of resistance.

Living in 2024, I see how the tribunal and the activist stories offer a framework for interpreting current social movements. Both show that today's movements are rooted in historical knowledge, emphasizing that change comes from a blend of awareness, persistence, and reclaiming narratives. The document and activist perspectives encourage us to see resistance not as isolated events but as a broader, interconnected movement that spans generations. They provide a lens through which we can interpret the present, recognizing the layers of struggle that define the social landscape. For me, this material speaks to the importance of solidarity and listening to under-represented voices. It suggests that engaging with historical and contemporary resistance narratives is essential in understanding the present and striving for a just future.

The 1992 Tribunal Verdict, the insights from the panelists, and the performance art pieces collectively deepen our understanding of resistance. They invite us to witness, remember, and respond to the cycles of oppression and resistance that shape history and contemporary movements. Together, they illuminate how resistance is not only about protesting against injustice, but also about sustaining a community, reclaiming identity, and passing on the legacy of resilience. Through this exploration, I see how understanding history empowers us to interpret the present with empathy, resolve, and the recognition that true justice requires continuity, unity, and a commitment to truth.

—Jonas Kramer

The International Tribunal Verdict: Still Guilty.

The front page of the verdict is a beautifully drawn piece of art titled in stark white against black and bold, "VERDICT OF THE INTERNATIONAL TRIBUNAL OF INDIGENOUS PEOPLES AND OPPRESSED NATIONS IN THE USA." There were only 1,000 copies of this second edition verdict made, printed on October 14th, 1992, just under two weeks after the International Tribunal met for the first time in San Francisco. The Verdict begins with an introduction about the convening of the International Tribunal in which activists, judges, journalists, and other community members from a mulit-racial coalitional front congregated to protest the celebration of Columbus' invasion. The verdict is a major document of the 1992 International Tribunal placing the United States of America on trial for its 'grave crimes against humanity, including representatives from several countries, including Spain, the Philippines, Germany, Puerto Rico, Hawaii, Haiti, South Africa, and Peru. A panel of distinguished judges, all experienced in human rights work, heard testimonies and deliberated for twelve hours, ultimately reaching a verdict that demanded the United States take accountability for its crimes.

The Tribunal organizers had three main goals. The first goal was to destroy the myth of Columbus and the 'European Discovery' of the Americas, halting a celebration of the colonization and horror that has plagued the land since Columbus's arrival, and declaring that Columbus didn't discover the Americas, which were already inhabited by thousands of Indigenous Tribes who already resided there. The second demand was Self Determination for Native Americans, Puerto Ricans, New Afrikans, and Mexicans. To have a full acknowledgement of the hundreds of years of genocide, racism, and colonialism. Lastly, they demanded the release of the hundreds of political prisoners of war from different activist movements, including Leonard Peltier, Eddie Hatcher, Norma Jean Croy, Alejandrina Torres, Oscar López, Geronimo Ji-Jaga, Mumia Abu Jamal, and Silvia Baraldini, all of whom were in U.S. prisons at the time (Verdict, 4).

It is such a rich document. Here are 15 pages, but I've truthfully barely scratched the surface, and there's so much information just in the first few pages alone. An entire book could be written on just this Tribunal and its verdict. Many of the names are not searchable, but some names are. Attorney Francisca Villalba Merino had only two or three articles written about her, two of which were published postmortem. I found no information on Dale Marie Standing Alone, nothing on Norbert Georg. However, I did find a great deal on the Society for Threatened Peoples, which is an NGO and human rights organization from Germany that campaigns against all forms of genocide and ethnocide. Mitsuye Yamada had a decent amount of information online, which was nice to see, as did Dr. Raye Richardson, and there was some information and works by Rory Snow Arrow Fausett. I found it interesting to research some of these names, figure out who they were, who is still alive, what they did with their lives outside of this document, the effect they had on the movement and on the world, and the many people they touched with their work. It was such an incredible honor to have those activists in the room with us.

I learned so much from Judith, Claude, and Arthur during the panel. The panel provided such a real perspective on everything we've been reading about, and it was an incredibly memorable experience. I feel like it gave a human context to the documents I've been studying. Though we did not touch on the Tribunal specifically during the panel, I was able to get a wider perspective of time and understanding. Listening to my classmates' questions and these panelists discussing their artifacts in depth allowed me to see the interconnectedness of these organizations and archives. It's easy to read words on a page when you're analyzing this kind of document, but having people live in the class — sharing their experiences and their knowledge — made the work, documents, and events connect for me. It was hard-hitting and inspiring most of all. This was recent, and sometimes it can be hard to get that perspective of realness and time without talking to someone who was actually there.

The panelists also made it incredibly local, drawing on the history of things they witnessed in Berkeley, the history of the city and the campus, and the reality of the oppression they witnessed. It was eye-opening: pieces of history in the Bay that I still knew so little about. I felt for a moment, transported back in time and simultaneously, very much in the present. I recall that Claude himself mentioned how he felt seeing the installation of a Sukkah by Sather Gate as he walked to the classroom. On the morning of this panel, I witnessed Berkeley UCPD take down the Sukkah for Palestine. They threw the sacred structure into the trash. It was non-violent, but equally violent in its way. I wanted to do more than just watch, so I found the courage to help them pull the branches of their Sukkah from the trash. I was shaking in anger and grief at the injustice I witnessed, but also in fear of the repercussions of speaking out, a fear that I wasn't unfamiliar with. It was nothing in comparison to the amount of courage that these brave activists have, both the ones I stand alongside today and the many of the past.

I imagined the amount of bravery it took to stand up to oppression on such a widespread level. I thought about the police brutality that we as a nation have witnessed for so many years. It made me reflect on the long history of police brutality, racism, genocide, injustice, and oppression existing here in the U.S., crimes that the United States of America has still not answered for. Despite organizations such as the International Tribunal demanding answers to these crimes through their verdict, answers and reparations have yet to come to fruition. Even with support for Palestine spread nationwide, the many protests full of citizens charging the United States with complicity in funding a genocide, the United States still refuses to acknowledge the verdicts of today.

I believe we are fighting the same battles today that our panelists and creators of this verdict were fighting in 1992. We, as a society, are forever affected by the horrors of genocide. The United States still has not taken proper accountability for the hundreds of years of trauma caused by colonialism. The United States is just as guilty now as it was then and has unfortunately only continued to add to the list of horrific crimes. If the Tribunal had met today and created a verdict representative of 2024, I believe it would only be longer. Certainly, one difference I am thankful to note is that there is more education on these topics, especially at UC Berkeley, because of the many activists who fought, some of whom even died, to advocate for these fields of study even to exist.

I find myself mourning a lot of what could have been, mourning that we are still fighting these battles, grieving all of the time that has gone by, and all of the change and growth that has yet to happen. It's hard to compare the past to the present when this past is still present; the fight never ended. Justice is never-ending, and activist voices are needed now more than ever.

—Alexander Marsh

Night of Resistance
Roots Against War
1991
Poster

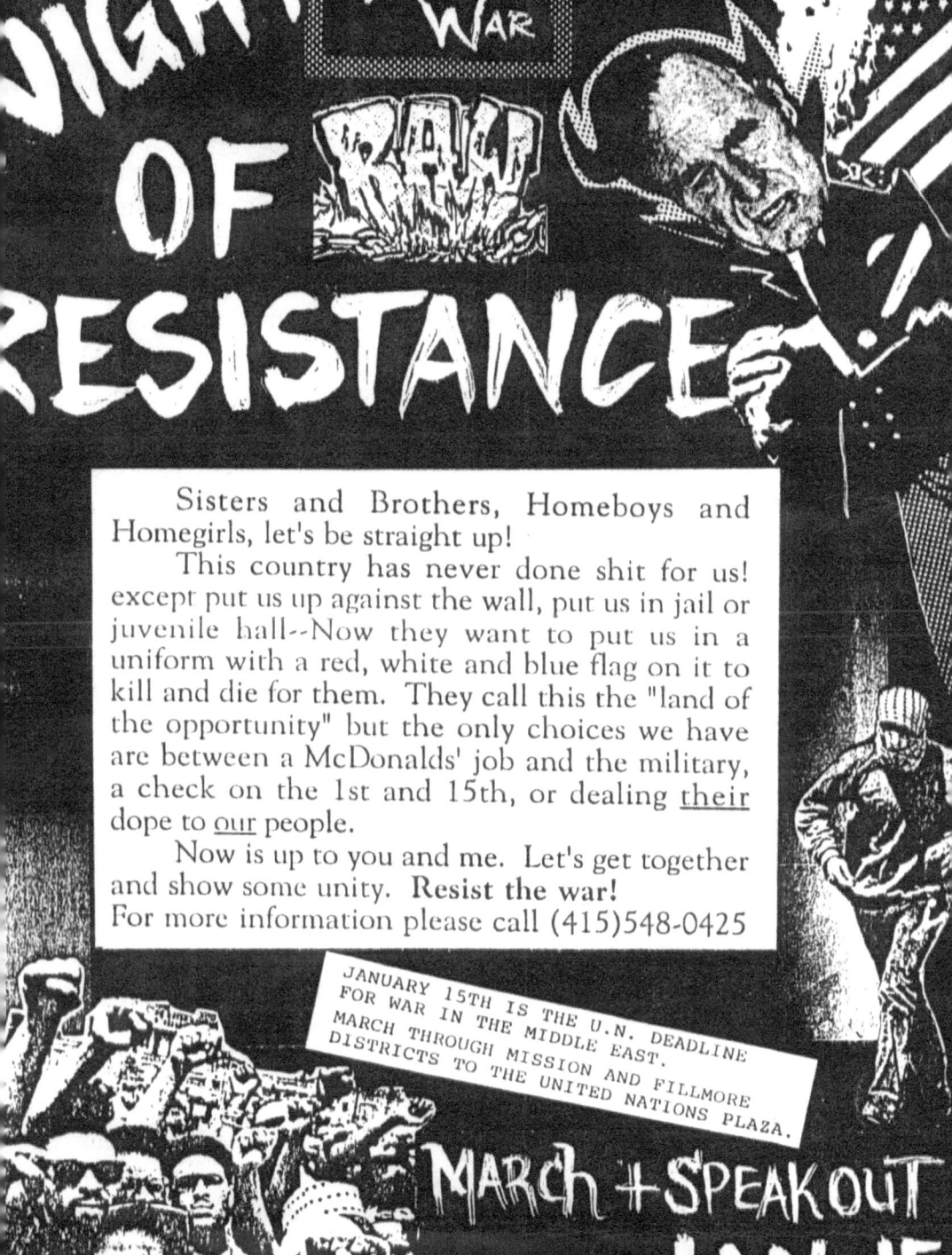

NIGHT OF RESISTANCE!

AGAINST WAR

RAW

Sisters and Brothers, Homeboys and Homegirls, let's be straight up!

This country has never done shit for us! except put us up against the wall, put us in jail or juvenile hall--Now they want to put us in a uniform with a red, white and blue flag on it to kill and die for them. They call this the "land of the opportunity" but the only choices we have are between a McDonalds' job and the military, a check on the 1st and 15th, or dealing their dope to our people.

Now is up to you and me. Let's get together and show some unity. **Resist the war!**

For more information please call (415)548-0425

JANUARY 15TH IS THE U.N. DEADLINE FOR WAR IN THE MIDDLE EAST.
MARCH THROUGH MISSION AND FILLMORE DISTRICTS TO THE UNITED NATIONS PLAZA.

MARCH + SPEAKOUT

Honor Martin
Luther King's
Anti-War Stance

JAN. 15
5:30 PM

Night of Resistance

The 1992 Tribunal brought together a coalitional front of activists and organizations, including groups like Roots Against War (RAW). Multi-racial and queer, RAW began as an anti-war, anti-imperialist, and anti-racist organization dedicated to ending poverty, unemployment, racial and gender discrimination, and police brutality in the 1990s. They were known for largely representing youth and women of color, artists, and activists of the greater Bay Area. Based in the heart of the Mission district of San Francisco, RAW organizers rallied thousands of people in Mission Dolores Park to protest the acquittal of four kops for the beating of Rodney King and imperial wars for oil profits. Massive arrests of demonstrators were common, and yet they continued to call for an end to the violence against people of color in the Bay and throughout the country.

The poster, "Night of Resistance," is an anti-war call for a march and open mic speakout held at the United Nations Plaza in San Francisco against the Iraq War of 1991. It is a youth shout of truth to expose the U.S.-UK-driven military offensive over oil, leading to 'Operation Desert Storm,' and the subsequent Iraq War. The poster draws essential connections between imperialist petroleum investments and impoverishment in the U.S., where young people of color are pipelined into the military, fast-food, or prison. The rally specifically called on the United Nations to de-escalate its ultimatum over Iraq's claims in a border dispute with Kuwait. Despite resistance on the ground, the U.S.-U.K. military launched 'Operation Desert Storm,' the beginning of a series of offensives that destroyed the infrastructure of Iraq, killing hundreds of thousands of people. A nod to Martin Luther King's Anti-War Stance is written at the bottom of the page.

Unabashedly queer, brown, and proud, RAW activists made this statement in the early 1990s:

"We lesbian/gay queer members of RAW do not support Bush's Gulf War. We cannot condone the spending of trillions of dollars for cheap oil, the destruction of Arab land, and genocidal acts against Arab people, or the disproportionate number of U.S. troops of color. Yet Bush still cuts welfare programs, housing, and education, and the U.S. government has yet to fund AIDS research and care adequately. In fact, in the first weeks of this war, the U.S. has spent more on funding its military machines of death than it has in a decade of AIDS research, treatment, and care! This is in a time when, if our lives continue to be declared expendable here and abroad, AIDS will soon be the number one killer of women and men of color. African Americans and Latinos make up 45 percent of people living with AIDS. Currently, Chicanos/Latinos make up 8 percent of the U.S. population, yet they are 14 percent of the HIV population. AIDS is the number one killer of African American women in New York City and nationwide; 50 percent of all women with AIDS are African Americans. Eighty percent of children born HIV-infected are African American. Ten percent of the Native American population is HIV positive, which is the size of many whole tribes. Filipinos are soon becoming San Francisco's largest HIV-positive group. And, on an international level, the presence of the U.S. military in the "Third World" has usually coincided with a high rate of HIV infection for Indigenous populations. We refuse to die for oil overseas, and we will not allow this government to neglect our lives within this country! Our people need education regarding safe sex and all forms of health care, rather than becoming pawns in Bush's oil war game. Queers of color cannot stand by and remain silent—we need to get on the streets with our love and our rage because, this being wartime, we are all at high risk. Roots Against War is an alliance of people of color dedicated to fighting this current war [and] the racist and sexist assaults on our communities, as well as [to] struggling with our people with regards to heterosexism and homophobia."[1]

1 Roots Against War, "Queers Get Raw!" (1991) in *Remaking Radicalism*, Dan Berger Ed., UP Georgia, 2020, p. 329.

RETHINKING COLUMBUS

TEACHING ABOUT THE 500TH ANNIVERSARY OF COLUMBUS'S ARRIVAL IN AMERICA

A SPECIAL ISSUE OF RETHINKING SCHOOLS

DEDICATED TO THE CHILDREN OF THE AMERICAS

Rethinking Columbus: Teaching about the 500th Anniversary of Columbus's Arrival in America
Cover Photo Pat Goudvis
1991

Periodical (Special Issue)

Rethinking Columbus

Muhammad Delgado

Rethinking Columbus is a special edition of the *Rethinking Schools* book series published in September 1991, in collaboration with the Network of Educators on Central America, just months ahead of the quincentennial. The Rethinking Schools group began in 1986 when a collective of teachers, educators, and community members in Milwaukee got together to bring critical perspectives into the national conversation about schools, libraries, and education to combat the country's prevalent conservative attitudes about pedagogy and curriculum. Their contributions to social justice in education included a quarterly tabloid that has been published continuously since its establishment in 1986. *Rethinking Columbus* was the group's first venture into publishing a full book.

Within its first month, *Rethinking Columbus* sold out all of its 30,000 copies, prompting a second printing in October 1991. The roughly one hundred-page book contains upwards of fifty articles, essays, poems, guides, historical documents, and other educational resources on the arrival of Columbus, colonization, genocide in the Americas, Indigenous cultures, and historical and contemporary resistance to colonialism. The book contains selections and contributions from educators, students, Native activists, and poets from across the U.S. and Indian country. The authors argue that the Columbus myth should be rethought and critiqued because of the foundational role it serves in shaping children's understanding of society.

The framing around Columbus in schools primes children to accept the core tenets of colonialism, imperialism, and racism by whitewashing genocide, erasing Native people and their experiences, and heroicizing colonizers and conquistadores. Whereas traditional American education has ignored marginalized perspectives and taught its pupils to do the same, *Rethinking Columbus* provides a forum for Native voices to articulate their experiences and stories. Across seven sections, its authors confront the iconic images of Columbus's discovery with extensive references to the point of view of Columbus's victims. Authors including Bill Bigelow and Jan Elliot call attention to crimes that have been committed against Indigenous people in both the earlier periods of colonization, by the expanding Spanish and American empires, as well as in the present under the federal government of the United States. These include—besides wanton slaughter, torture, and enslavement—the violation of Native land rights, the violation of Native rights to sovereignty and self-determination, and other treacherous means of undermining Native life.

Moreover, the authors of this volume do not merely portray Native people as victims of the specter of colonization, but instead acknowledge their agency and their living place in history and the present. Many of the texts included in the book, such as Deborah Menkart's article on Guatemala titled "Indians Fight Modern Conquistadores," discuss contemporary resistance, demonstrating the living legacy of the genocide and the struggle against it. Furthermore, attention is called to the generative, creative qualities of Native life that exist without or despite colonization. For example, an "Alphabet of Things that the Americas Gave to the World," and a number of poems recenter the conversation about Indigenous communities away from what Eve Tuck terms: the "damage-based framework" that usually pervades all discourse about Native peoples. The book also dedicates space to Latin American and African American perspectives on Columbus.

Rethinking Columbus had an influential role in changing how schools taught about Columbus in many parts of the country. In 2003, the group published an expanded second edition of *Rethinking Columbus*, subtitled "The Next 500 Years" and fitted with over a hundred new pages of essays, poems, interviews, historical vignettes, and lesson plans that expand upon the marginalized stories of the 500 years of struggle since 1492.

Solidarity with Haiti Against U.S. Imperialism

Haiti Action Committee, www.haitisolidarity.net

In 1791, four-hundred thousand Africans enslaved in Haiti rose up against French colonial rule. They launched a revolutionary war that culminated in Haiti's independence in 1804, establishing the world's first Black republic. From that moment on, Haiti has been a guiding star of liberation, while also in the crosshairs of white supremacist imperial powers. Knowing that Haiti was an inspiration to enslaved people everywhere, the United States led a worldwide boycott and refused to recognize the new republic until 1862. In 1915, the U.S. invaded Haiti and occupied the country for nineteen years, taking over Haiti's banking system, repressing a peasant-led insurgency, and installing one puppet regime after another, culminating with the Duvalier dictatorships which terrorized the country for close to thirty years.

After decades of organizing, a massive grassroots movement of Haiti's impoverished majority, known as Lavalas, was able to non-violently overthrow the US-backed Duvalier as well as the succeeding military dictatorship and elect the popular priest Jean-Bertrand Aristide as President in 1990. Less than a year later, the U.S. retaliated and installed another military reign of terror. Despite thousands of murders, Lavalas continued to resist and President Aristide returned to Haiti in 1994. He was elected again in 2000, and demanded restitution of the ransom for recognition of Haiti's independence extorted by France.

During Aristide's brief time in office, more schools were built than the total constructed between 1804 and 1994. Twenty percent of the country's budget was mandated for education. Women's groups and popular organizations helped coordinate a literacy campaign that brought over 320,000 people, mostly women, into literacy classes in over 20,000 literacy centers. The minimum wage was doubled. Health clinics were established in the poorest communities. Yet, in 2004, the democratically-elected government of the Fanmi Lavalas party was once again overthrown by a violent US-backed coup. The country's democratic system and social gains were shattered, leading to paramilitary violence and mass emigration. Despite this, knowing of their power, the people of Haiti teach the world what it means to be resilient, continuing a legacy of resistance to imperialism.

MUMIA ABU JAMAL FACES IMMINENT EXECUTION

The State of Pennsylvania has accelerated its efforts to legally lynch former Black Panther Party member and MOVE supporter Mumia Abu Jamal. It is expected that Pennsylvania Governor Robert Casey will soon decide whether to sign the death warrant for Mumia, a move which would set the stage for the first overtly political execution in the United States since the re-institution of the death penalty in 1976.

Mumia became a radio journalist in the 1970's, earning the title "The Voice of the Voiceless" in Philadelphia. Outraged by the racist brutalization of the MOVE organization, Mumia became a vocal supporter of MOVE, which led to increased police harassment from the Philadelphia Police Department. On December 9, 1981, Mumia and his brother were attacked by the police, in an incident which left one police officer dead. Mumia was tried and convicted of murder.

During the sentencing phase of his trail, the District Attorney argued that Mumia's 1960's membership in the Black Panther Party, and his support for that organizations platform of armed self defense, warranted imposition of the death penalty. The jury agreed, and Mumia was sentenced to death. All legal appeals have been exhausted, and Mumia is #1 on Pennsylvania's lest of individuals awaiting executions. A national and international campaign has been organized to save Mumia, and demand his release from jail.

Call or write **IMMEDIATELY** to: Governor Casey, Main Capitol Building Room 225, Harrisburg, PA 16652.

❀❀

For more information, contact Concerned Friends and Family of Mumia Abu Jamal, P.O. Box 19709, Philadelphia, PA 19143, (215) 552-8985. Support work is also being conducted by Equal Justice, U.S.A. / Quixote Center, P.O. Box 5206, Hyattsville, MD 20782, the Ad Hoc Coalition for Mumia Abu Jamal, 2170 Broadway - Suite 2234, New York, NY 10024, (212) 740-8557, and the Campaign to Free Black Political Prisoners and POWs, at (718) 624-0800. Contributions may be made to the Black United Fund (with checks made out to BUF/MA Jamal Fund), 419 South 15 Street, Philadelphia, PA 19145. Write to: Mumia Abu Jamal, #AM-8335, Drawer R, Huntingdon PA 16652.

Free Mumia Abu Jamal

Joaquin Min Antonio

Mumia Abu Jamal's struggle for freedom is displayed as the centerpiece in "Diss'ing the 'Discovery': Political Prisoners and Prisoners of War in U.S. Prisons, De-Celebrate the Columbus Quincentenary and affirm 500 years of Resistance," a booklet released during the 1992 Tribunal and digitally preserved in the Freedom Archives. Mumia Abu Jamal is a well-renowned African American radio journalist, writer, and activist fighting for freedom from political imprisonment of over 44 years.

After experiencing police brutality as a young teenager, Mumia became politically active and helped found the Pennsylvania branch of the Black Panther Party in 1968 at the age of 14. He developed into a prolific revolutionary journalist and propagandist, writing articles with agitating calls and messages for the Black Panther, the newspaper of the Black Panther Party. As the Lieutenant of Information for the Philadelphia branch of the party, he also wrote leaflets, press releases, and pamphlets, spoke at events and ceremonies, and performed common party political tasks like supporting the free breakfast program for Black children. His activism with the Black Panther Party was so pronounced that it attracted the attention of the FBI, and he alongside many of his comrades were put on surveillance lists.

As the Black Panther Party faced relentless state attacks and eventual decline, Mumia would continue to utilize his journalism skills as a radio operator by revealing the daily struggles faced by Black working-class people. His exposé on police brutality and anti-Black racism made him famous throughout the Philadelphia area. He garnered much praise in the journalist community, eventually becoming president of the Philadelphia chapter of the Association of Black Journalists.

Mumia never let prestige drown his dedication to his people, and he would continue to cover people's movements like the MOVE organization in the late 1970s and early 1980s. MOVE's struggle for Black self-determination and social justice was not tolerated by the racist and corrupt Philadelphia Police Department, prompting multiple police sieges and standoffs with the organization. During the infamous 1978 police standoff with MOVE members, it was Mumia who helped disclose that it was the police, not MOVE, who killed one of their own officers in friendly fire. Mumia's defense of MOVE only further attracted the reactionary agitation of the conservative elite and Philadelphia police.

In 1981, Mumia was framed for the murder of a police officer. After having been pushed out of his radio show for his unwavering political journalism, he started to drive a taxi cab. One night, after hearing gunshots, he witnessed his brother being harassed by police. The police soon turned their attention to Mumia, shooting and beating him. One police officer was left dead by an unknown perpetrator, but Mumia was never tested for gunshot residue, and eyewitness accounts vary drastically in story and reliability. Nonetheless, the police department left Mumia in critical condition and rushed to convict him of murder.

The Philadelphia Police Department ruthlessly displays how deeply rooted white supremacy is in American institutions. The department had long been criticized for over-policing Black neighborhoods and murdering Black men. Long-time Police Commissioner and Mayor, Frank Rizzo, put targets on the backs of Black people and systematized their brutalization. Furthermore, the overt corruption within the department symbolizes the mafia-esque style in which their officers work. At the time of Mumia's conviction, over 30 police officers from the precinct that had arrested him were indicted for corruption and other scandals. Even after his arrest, Mumia was convicted and given a death sentence by the infamous judge Albert Sabo and a racist jury with only two Black jurors. Albert Sabo would end up sentencing over 31 people to death, the most of any judge in Pennsylvania.

The arrest and conviction of Mumia is a frame-up to punish him for his history of militant activism and pro-people journalism. While imprisoned, he remained steadfast in challenging the ruling class and fighting for his freedom. Mumia remained on death row for 30 years until 2011, when he was victorious in overturning the prosecutor's attempts to uphold his death sentence. Though he remains wrongfully imprisoned to a life sentence term, he has published a plethora of books and still publishes statements of solidarity for oppressed people around the world from prison. Recently, his son, Jamal Ibn Mumia, has led Mumia Freedom Tours to spread the message: Mumia is innocent and framed!

Throughout the Diss'ing the 'Discovery' booklet, Mumia is prominently highlighted alongside Leonard Peltier as two political prisoners demanding their freedom. Leonard's recent release in February is not only a welcoming victory for his people and Indigenous peoples around Turtle Island, but also marks a near victory for other political prisoners and those fighting for the liberation of their people like Mumia Abu Jamal.

The 1992 Tribunal also reached a conviction: the United States is guilty of continuing the 500 years of white supremacist colonialism, occupation, and genocide. The 1992 Tribunal highlighted people's movements and made calls to release prisoners of war engaged in struggles for national liberation. Demanding the release of Mumia Abu Jamal back in 1992 was only a single snapshot of the 44-year-long struggle for his freedom. Though Mumia won in his fight against the brutal death sentence, he remains imprisoned in San Quentin for a crime he did not commit and for fighting for the liberation of Black people. Similarly, Indigenous people of Turtle Island have continued to face occupation and genocide for over 533 years. Join the struggle and spread the word to FREE MUMIA and decolonize Turtle Island!

Tribunal Project: Voices Set Free 2024-25

"When a man dies from a hanging tree, is that tree an accessory to the act or a witness? Could these magnificent and venerable forest giants be gifted with a descriptive historical tongue—how their recital would startle us."
-Author Unknown

Elevating Indigenous and Mexican Perspectives on California's History
The Tribunal Project is embarking on a transformative mission to reshape the historical narrative of California's colonial past by centering Indigenous and Mexican/Mexican-American voices. With a focus on the 21st Mission in Sonoma Valley, California, this initiative seeks to convert the site into a Site of Consciousness, bringing public attention to the overlooked atrocities and resilience of these communities.

Challenging Dominant Narratives
For too long, the historical discourse surrounding California's missions has been dominated by the Spanish colonial perspective, often neglecting the suffering and resistance of Indigenous peoples. The Tribunal Project aims to counter these exclusionary narratives, emphasizing the resilience and agency of Indigenous and Mexican/Mexican-American communities in shaping California's history.

Objectives of the Tribunal Project
- Reclaiming Historical Narratives – The initiative challenges dominant perspectives on Spain's Mission System by highlighting the often-ignored voices of Indigenous and Mexican-American communities.
- Fostering Critical Engagement – By addressing themes such as social reproduction, racial capitalism, and state power, the project fosters a deeper public understanding of colonial histories and their modern-day ramifications.
- Reimagining the Politics of Care – The Tribunal Project explores new frameworks for care and social justice, advocating for egalitarian, anti-capitalist forms of collective action and mutual aid.

A Multi-Faceted Approach to Transformation

The Tribunal Project employs a multi-pronged strategy to achieve its goals, ensuring that research, dialogue, and public engagement remain at the heart of the initiative:

- **Collaborative Research** – Scholars, historians, and community leaders will conduct in-depth research on the impacts of the California missions on Indigenous and Mexican-American communities.
- **Seminar Series** – A series of discussions, workshops, and panels will engage participants in critical inquiry into colonial history, racial capitalism, and social justice.
- **Community Engagement** – Working with Indigenous leaders and grassroots organizations, the project will integrate the voices and aspirations of those most affected by historical injustices.
- **Public Awareness Campaign** – Through the Tradition of storytelling, educational resources, and multimedia efforts, the project will raise awareness and encourage public discourse on the need to confront and reclaim historical memory.

A Lasting Impact on Historical Memory and Justice

Through its bold re-examination of California's history, the Tribunal Project aspires to:

- **Provide** a more inclusive and accurate representation of California's past.
- **Honor** the resilience and ongoing struggle of Indigenous and Mexican-American communities.
- **Inspire** new avenues for collective action and justice-oriented organizing.

The Tribunal Project is an urgent call to action for scholars, activists, and community members dedicated to historical justice and liberation. By reclaiming narratives and amplifying marginalized voices, this initiative paves the way for a more equitable and conscious future.   tribunalproject.org

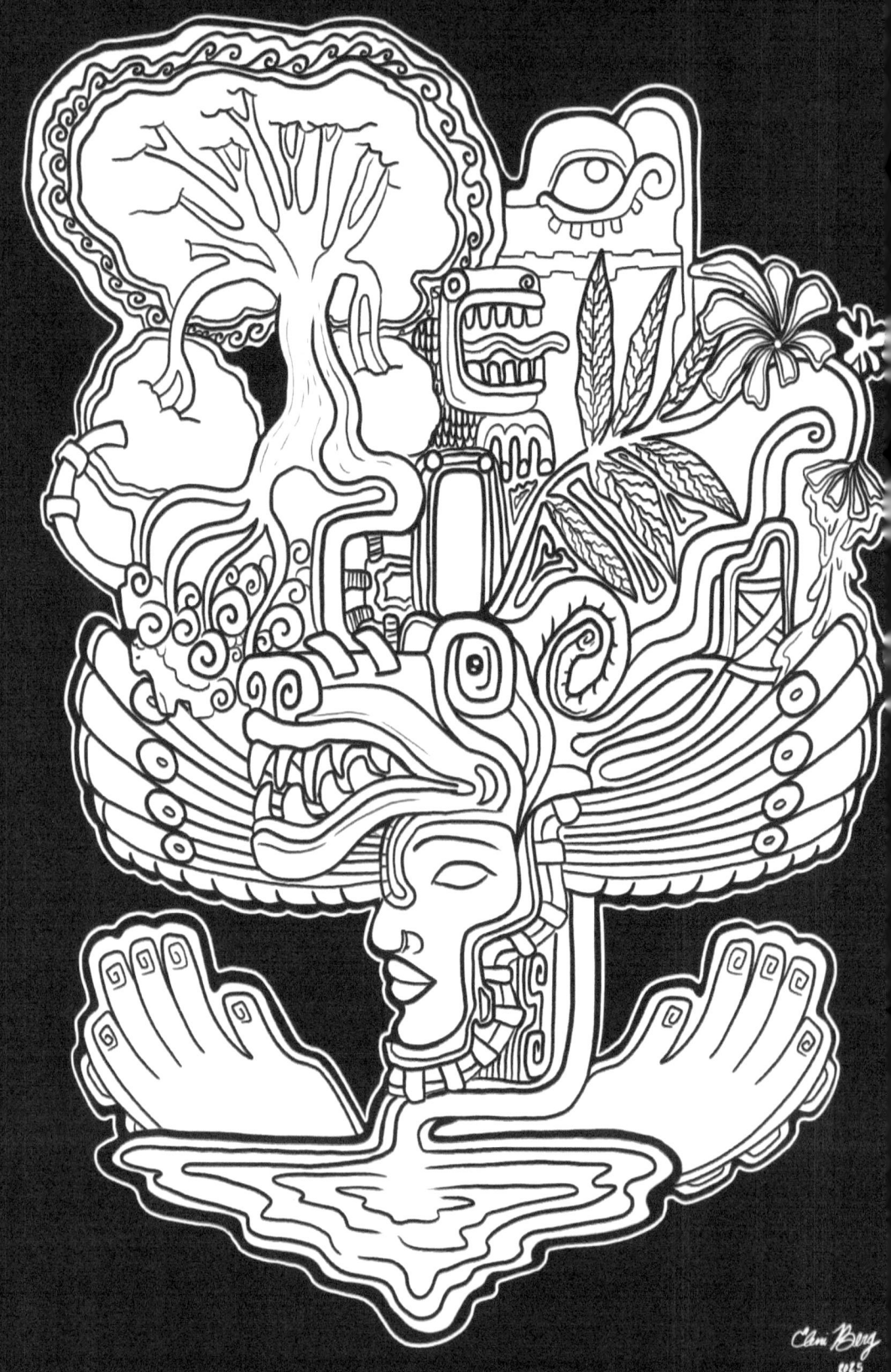

PART THREE:
TRIBUNAL FRAMEWORKS
CRITIQUE AND CREATE

The People v The U.S.-Narco State of Juan Orlando Hernandez

Lulu Matute[1]

From 2010 to 2022, the United States government collaborated with a politically corrupt, drug-trafficking regime in Honduras—a regime it helped install and continued to support even as evidence of criminality mounted. Over time, that relationship unraveled, implicating former presidents, police chiefs, and a vast network of drug transport, bribes, and assassinations. On March 8, 2024, former Honduran president Juan Orlando Hernández (JOH) was convicted in U.S. federal court, along with his brother, a cousin in the National Police, and former president Porfirio Lobo, for their roles in a drug and arms trafficking conspiracy. This conspiracy was sustained by U.S. foreign policy, which provided funding, military training, and diplomatic legitimacy.

Next to the plentiful accolades, photo ops, and official public statements exuberantly shared between this Honduran narco-regime and the current U.S. Secretary of State, then-Senator Marco Rubio, the full extent of this charge has yet to be uncovered. The U.S. trial, the conviction, and especially the official relationship with JOH were scarcely reported and in fact, scrubbed from public Internet records to protect Marco Rubio, the State Department, and U.S. military aggression in the region. While the U.S. Department of Justice framed the extradition and conviction of JOH as a victory for the rule of law, the case and the reception of such a verdict by the U.S. State Department omitted a critical truth: the United States was not solely an observer, it was JOH's chief enabler, aiding and abetting the trafficking of tons of cocaine and firearms including financing a regime that they installed for nearly a decade.

In the coverage of the U.S. so-called War Against Drugs by the mainstream media, there is little to any exposure of Rubio's and the Department of Defense's tight relationships with the narco regime, nor about the U.S. network of police and military infrastructure that was used for the deadly narco operation. This pattern of propaganda against socialist states, most prominently

1 Contributions to this article were made by a team of researchers of the D+M Lab. Special thanks to the School of the Americas Watch organizers and support.

Section

now Venezuela, is on repeat cycle.[2] The U.S. projects a battery of baseless charges to distract from and conceal its complicity, with the mainstream media dutifully reciting these charges while failing to investigate and bring to the light the full criminality of US officials.

On March 6, 2024, U.S. prosecutor Jacob Gutwillig declared before a federal court in New York: "The defendant [Juan Orlando Hernández] was the President of Honduras, but in the end, he's just a drug dealer who sent massive amounts of cocaine to this country. Hold him accountable, find him guilty." [3] These closing remarks framed the trial as a straightforward case of justice served. Yet the U.S. government omits its own role in empowering JOH—not as a rogue actor, but as a strategic ally. For over a decade, the U.S. provided political cover and military support to JOH's authoritarian regime. With the State Department and then-Florida Senator Marco Rubio's backing, JOH consolidated power, repressed opposition, and facilitated the looting of Honduras' resources by corporate interests[4]. While U.S. officials, including Rubio, showered visits and business deals with the now-convicted statesman, JOH transformed the country into a narco-state, weaponizing U.S. -funded security forces for his authoritarianism. By the end of his rule, Honduras' poverty and violence had escalated, forcing mass migration northward—a crisis the U.S. now criminalizes while conveniently ignoring its own role in creating it.

The People's Tribunal framework allows us to look beyond JOH's trial and even his conviction to the erasure that serves U.S. imperialism. The U.S. frames JOH's conviction as a triumph in the "War on Drugs," but the whole story reveals Washington's complicity in legitimizing JOH precisely while he was engaged in trafficking operations, including active relationships with major cartels. What we charge is that the U.S. State Department, now headed by Rubio, engages in willful deception regarding this case to whitewash decades of U.S. intervention in Honduras. The U.S. violated Hon-

2 For a detailed review of U.S. complicity in the 1980s, see Peter Dale Scott and Jonathan Marshall in *Cocaine Politics: Drugs, Armies, and the CIA in Cental America*. California UP, 1991.

3 https://www.justice.gov/archives/opa/pr/juan-orlando-hernandez-former-president-honduras-sentenced-45-years-prison-conspiring https://www.hondurasnow.org/day-twelve-joh-finished-testifying-court-heard-closing-remarks-the-trial-has-ended

4 https://ips-dc.org/report-corporate-assault-on-honduras/

duran sovereignty by endorsing JOH's regime despite its undemocratic and unconstitutional capture of power in Honduras. Without acknowledging the complicity of the relationship to JOH, the U.S. trial and conviction of their former ally ultimately served to cover up the full depth of the crime. The U.S. practice of strategic omission of facts or a selective truth-telling before and post JOH's conviction is evidence of systemic abuse of power. This article adopts the lens of a Peoples Tribunal, examining the U.S. as a co-conspirator in JOH's crimes and exposing how the "War on Drugs" narrative is further weaponized to justify illegal foreign intervention in the affairs of sovereign nations and other autonomous territories of the Global South.

U.S. Interests leading up to the 2009 Coup

Honduras has long been a U.S. military outpost. Its relationship to Washington as a 'banana republic' was for decades marked by open repression and corruption in the highest offices conducted by U.S. agents. Yet the U.S. attributes the country's instability to local corruption—erasing its own role and exploitative history. To only summarily name a few of the most notable parts of this history, we remember that in 1953, President Dwight Eisenhower appointed John Foster Dulles as the Secretary of State and Allen Dulles as the director of the Central Intelligence Agency (CIA). The brothers also served as legal advisers to the United Fruit Company's operations in the region. The following year, in 1954, the Dulles brothers collaborated to overthrow the democratically elected socialist president of Guatemala, Jacobo Arbenz.[5] From that point forward, the U.S. government continued to use Honduras as a base to launch the CIA-organized coup in Guatemala, contributing to the state-sponsored genocide against the Guatemalan people. The 1954 CIA-organized coup in Guatemala, along with its utilization of Honduras for counterinsurgency operations, also played a role in suppressing a 69-day general strike in Honduras. The Dulles brothers worked to quickly militarize the country and quell uprisings within labor and peasant movements in Honduras.[6]

This clear connection between the U.S. government departments and

5 https://www.ft.com/content/778739c4-f869-11db-a940-000b5df10621
6 Dana Frank, 2018.

agencies, particularly the CIA and the Secretary of State, and their ties to U.S. banana companies United Fruit Company (now Chiquita) and the Standard Fruit Company (now Dole), played, and still play, a significant role in establishing covert and overt military operations in Central America. The alignment of interests between the U.S. government and corporate executives prioritizes the protection of company assets and financial interests over workers, environmental protections, and human rights. Meanwhile, U.S. funding supplied Honduran proxy wars aimed at preventing people from organizing in their own self-defense and self-determination. In their rabid terror campaign against people's movements, the U.S. government converted Honduras into its main base for U.S. counterintelligence operations throughout Latin America.[7][8]

Built in 1981, Soto Cano Air Base, also known as Palmerola, became the chief U.S. military air base in Honduras and the largest U.S. military base in Latin America.[9] Its construction solidified the ongoing political and military relationships between U.S. and Honduran elites, particularly following the Nicaraguan revolution of 1979.[10] With the explicit aim to control populations and eliminate socialist and communist movements, including land and water defenders, the Soto Cano Air Base became a geopolitical asset for U.S. influence. Funding locked in economic dependence. Supplies were delivered. Palmerola is a well-known militarized fort for U.S. air and ground control over the Western hemisphere, a power dynamic based on the logic of the Monroe Doctrine.[11]

During this time, the U.S. government provided training, equipment, and funding to Battalion 3-16, one of the most notorious death squads respon-

7   "Reagan Doctrine, 1985," *U.S. Department of State*. January 20, 2009. https://2001-2009.state.gov/r/pa/ho/time/rd/17741.htm.

8   "Honduras," *The Center for Justice & Accountability*. https://cja.org/where-we-work/honduras/

9   Beau Downy. "A History of Joint Task Force-Bravo," *Joint Task Force-Bravo*, April 7, 2020. https://www.jtfb.southcom.mil/Portals/14/documents/A%20History%20of%20 JTF-Bravo.pdf?ver=2020-04-07-122737-510&timestamp=1586276868596

10   Beau Downy. "A History of Joint Task Force-Bravo," *Joint Task Force-Bravo*, April 7, 2020. https://www.jtfb.southcom.mil/Portals/14/documents/A%20History%20of%20 JTF-Bravo.pdf?ver=2020-04-07-122737-510&timestamp=1586276868596

11   See Shaka Shakur for the term 'militarized fort' in reference to the outgrowth of massive cop cities in the U.S. See full text of Monroe Doctrine here for the pretense of 'protection' from other colonizing nations: https://www.archives.gov/milestone-documents/monroe-doctrine

sible for torture, abductions, and executions of Honduran civilians. Battalion 3-16's orders were purportedly to target arms traffickers to Salvadoran guerrillas, yet were explicitly designed for the extermination of what the regime called 'communists,' supported by extensive cooperation between the Reagan administration and the Honduran military.[12] In 1995, The Baltimore Sun published a comprehensive four-part series that drew upon interviews conducted with Florencio Caballero, a former member of Battalion 3-16, and survivors of torture in Honduras. These interviews collectively revealed a portrayal of human rights abuses funded by U.S. taxpayers and exposed the CIA's role in the operations of Battalion 3-16.[13] Later reports confirm that Battalion 3-16 functioned as a death squad under the command of Honduran military officers and graduates of the U.S. Army School of the Americas, General Álvarez Martínez and Lt. Col. Juan López Grijalba.[14] Training programs conducted by the School of the Americas, CIA, and FBI for Honduran military officers in interrogation and surveillance included funding of Argentine counterinsurgency experts who trained "anti-communist" forces. The battalion collected intelligence on suspected political opponents of the government and targeted political activists, which included students, teachers, farmers, and unionists.[15] Individuals were killed or at risk of being forcibly disappeared to silence anyone suspected by the military of being a political dissident.[16]

In addition to killings internal to Honduras, the United States once again converted the country into a strategic base for launching offensives against neighboring Nicaragua by the establishment of numerous airfields, supply depots, and base camps. The Iran-Contra affair, a scandal that unfolded during the Reagan administration in the mid-1980s, serves as a pivotal illustration of the geopolitical and neo-colonial dynamics at play in Honduras. At its core,

12 "The Truth America Owes Honduras," *The New York Times*, October 9, 1995, https://www.nytimes.com/1995/10/09/opinion/the-truth-america-owes-honduras.html

13 Gary Cohn and Ginger Thompson, "When a Wave of Torture an Murder Staggered a Small U.S. Ally, Truth was a Casualty," *The Baltimore Sun*, June 11, 1995, https://webcitation.org/5j6KNYW6F.

14 "Notorious SOA Graduates from Honduras," *School of the Americas Watch*. March 6, 2019. https://soaw.org/notorious-soa-graduates-from-honduras.

15 Sources: The Center for Justice & Accountability ; SOAW Notorious SOA Graduates from Honduras

16 See https://www.amnesty.org/fr/wp-content/uploads/2021/06/amr370021992en.pdf

it involved the secret sale of U.S. arms to Iran, with the proceeds illegally funneled to support the Contras, a U.S.-backed counter-insurgency group in Nicaragua fighting the Sandinista government despite a Congressional ban on such aid. The responsibility for this operation involved the rotation of numerous regular U.S. military and National Guard units on duty in Honduras, underlining its strategic importance to U.S. geopolitical interests,[17] Moreover, independent analysts tie these mobilizations to Honduras as a major drug transit point, long within the purview of U.S. officials in what they call a 'cocaine-military symbiosis.'[18] U.S. funding not only increased the operational capabilities of Honduran security forces but also trained elite military units directly involved in human rights abuses during this period.

The Iran-Contra scandal and its unresolved consequences underscore the extent to which Honduras has been used as a neocolonial pawn with little to no measure of accountability within or outside the U.S. While several officials were convicted for their roles in the scandal, many convictions were later vacated or pardoned in the final days of the Reagan presidency and the beginning of George H.W. Bush's term, including infamous warmonger Elliot Abrams, who was pardoned in 1992.[19]

Human rights abuses in Honduras were recorded, and with full knowledge of the U.S. State Department and other officials. As per a report from the CIA inspector general in 1997, officials from the United States stationed in Honduras were cognizant of significant human rights violations committed by the Honduran military but did not accurately report this to Congress. Several reports by journalists and the Center for Justice and Accountability called out the ongoing pattern of human rights abuses from the 1980s, 1990s, and early 2000s, and yet they were largely ignored. Records obtained from the U.S. from as early as 1981 were extensively redacted, revealing the suppression of information by the U.S. Embassy during Negroponte's tenure,[20] and the decades-long pattern that continued of secrecy, withholding of the full

17 "The Iran-Contra Affair 20 Years On," *The National Security Archive*, November 24, 2006, https://nsarchive2.gwu.edu/NSAEBB/NSAEBB210/.
18 See Dale and Marshall, 1991.
19 https://caselaw.findlaw.com/court/dc-court-of-appeals/1280741.html
20 "Nomination of John Negroponte to Represent the U.S. at the United Nations," *GovInfo*, September 14, 2001, https://www.govinfo.gov/content/pkg/CREC-2001-09-14/html/CREC-2001-09-14-pt1-PgS9461-6.htm

truth from Congress and the American public.[21] The U.S. military Southern Command's (SOUTHCOM) narrative of democratic triumph in Central America thus comes as no surprise and yet is disingenuous given the relatively unchanging profile of U.S. foreign policy, military command, and unbridled economic interests in Honduras. Instead of marking the end of the Cold War and the beginning of a new era of democracy, the 2009 military coup and the undemocratic rise to power of U.S. ally Juan Orlando Hernández perpetuated ongoing abuse, criminal behaviors, reasoning, and denial.

In the lead-up to the coup, democratically elected President Manuel Zelaya had introduced significant domestic reforms aimed at improving the well-being of Hondurans.[22] These policies included free public education for youth, raising the average minimum wages by 60%,[23] and progressive social welfare measures like cash transfers and free electricity to help reduce absolute poverty.[24] Additionally, as labor and social movement historian Dana Frank analyzes in *The Long Honduran Night*, Zelaya "opened the door to restoring the land rights of small farmers, and, most importantly, stopped multiple power grabs by the elites, who sought to privatize publicly owned ports, education system, electrical system, and anything else they could get their hands on."[25]

President Zelaya engaged in discussions with left-wing social movements in Honduras that were critical of the U.S. military presence. Many of these groups advocated for a *constituyente*, an elected constituent assembly that, if assembled, would have been tasked with crafting a more progressive iteration of the 1982 Honduran constitution, which was formulated and adopted under the coercive influence of U.S.-funded Cold War operations in Cen-

21 "Honduras," *The Center for Justice & Accountability.* https://cja.org/where-we-work/honduras/

22 See https://thetricontinental.org/wp-content/uploads/2021/04/20210408_Dossier-39_EN_Web.pdf

23 Andres Ham, "Should developing countries increase their minimum wages?" November 28, 2016, https://blogs.worldbank.org/impactevaluations/should-developing-countries-increase-their-minimum-wages-guest-post-andr-s-ham#:~:text=Second%2C%20President%20Manuel%20Zelaya%20raised,equalize%20minimum%20wages%20across%20categories

24 See https://thetricontinental.org/wp-content/uploads/2021/04/20210408_Dossier-39_EN_Web.pdf

25 See Dana Frank, 2018.

tral America.[26] Zelaya's choice to hold a non-binding poll, asking Hondurans whether the issue of the constitutional assembly should be included in the upcoming elections, served as the contentious pretext for the 2009 military coup. Despite lacking substantiated evidence, Zelaya's opponents accused him of trying to amend the constitution to extend his presidency indefinitely. They collaborated with the top two U.S.-trained Honduran military generals, the aforementioned General Vásquez-Velásquez and General Prince-Suazo, to unlawfully remove and exile Zelaya before the *constituyente* referendum could occur.[27] On June 28, 2009, the democratically elected President of Honduras, Manuel Zelaya, was deposed from his position in a military coup d'état led by U.S.-trained Honduran military generals.

To bring this consequence into sharper view, between 2009 and 2024, hundreds of thousands of Hondurans were exiled.[28] Environmental defenders like Berta Cáceres were gunned down, and Garifuna leaders like Miriam Miranda were beaten, arrested, and criminalized. Indigenous communities were displaced to make way for extractive mega-projects and further destruction of rivers and arable lands. Since the U.S.-backed coup, following decades of infrastructural and institutional development of this outpost of imperialism, the architects of this regime in Honduras were trained, funded, and politically protected by the United States. This alliance was no accident, and this story is not just about the fall of a corrupt president. It is a case study in U.S. foreign policy hypocrisy—a state willing to prosecute its former ally while concealing its own role in arming, financing, and legitimizing his regime. What emerges is not merely complicity—but strategic collaboration. The U.S. prioritized regional dominance over democracy, especially as "nearshoring" (shifting supply chains from China) began to strengthen the capacity of southern neighbors to withstand and survive U.S. imperialist aggression.[29] By backing the post-2009 coup government, the U.S. actively participated in

---

26 See https://nacla.org/news/2018/03/13/dirty-elections-honduras-washington%E2%80%99s-blessing

27 See Dana Frank, 2018.

28 https://www.wola.org/wp-content/uploads/2023/06/2023-06_honduras_report.pdf

29 https://features.csis.org/US-nearshoring-in-central-america-with-SEZs/; See also https://www.bakerinstitute.org/research/60-years-nearshoring-historical-exploration-us-production-shifting-mexico

dismantling Honduran democracy and enabling the exploitation of its natural resources and cheap labor both within and outside of Honduras' borders. Furthermore, we can identify the active erasure or "scrubbing" of the relationship between U.S. officials and the Honduran political elite. Today, Rubio is the Secretary of State, and his ties to JOH are officially erased from the public record.

We indict the United States government for its role in facilitating and legitimizing the transformation of Honduras into a narco-state. From endorsing the 2009 coup, to legitimizing the elections that followed, to funding military operations used to terrorize the population, the U.S. government is culpable in the political destabilization and forced displacement of the Honduran people, which has caused cumulative suffering and damage for generations.

As the facts of the case led to the conviction of the former President, the previous relationships that endorsed and financially supported JOH were left unscrutinized. Why did U.S. prosecutors fail to investigate this crucial element of the case: **the role the U.S. government played in JOH's rise, tenure, and impunity?** Since the U.S. indictment of JOH, no State Department official, no agency, and no congressional hearing has addressed how U.S. political, military, and financial support enabled JOH to transform Honduras into a repressive authoritarian narco-state. What court will address such an obvious and wrongful crime? What this case brings forward is how issues of jurisdiction are, by imperial design, strategies to silo information, omit what is obvious, and ultimately chop and extract the case from its historical lineage. To counteract this, we see the conviction of JOH as not the end of the story—it is the beginning of a broader reckoning. This People's Indictment charges not only the individual, but the institutional failure to address the systemic violations that made JOH's rule possible.

In explaining JOH's extradition to the U.S., Anne Milgram DEA Administrator, slipped to signal the broader impact of financial corruption:

"Juan Orlando Hernandez, the former President of Honduras, was a central figure in one of the largest and most violent cocaine-trafficking conspiracies in the world. Hernandez used drug-trafficking proceeds to finance his political ascent and, once elected President, leveraged the Government of Honduras' law enforcement, military,

and financial resources to further his drug-trafficking scheme."[30]
Yet, what Milgram did not say was that those very institutions—the military, the police, and the financial apparatus—were strengthened with U.S. aid and shielded by U.S. diplomatic support.

The guilty pleas of Tony Hernández, Pineda, Bonilla, and others, who all stood trial—alongside JOH's conviction—only begin to uncover the scale of interstate criminality that has primarily used National Police and Army vehicles, highways, and political cover for its operations. The evidence shows that, following the 2009 coup, Honduras was restructured not just into an authoritarian client state, but into a logistics corridor for transnational drug trafficking.

Inspired by the model of The Permanent People's Tribunal,[31] this indictment does not rely on the authority of states but on the collective memory and lived experience of the people. "The People" includes: Honduran citizens whose families were torn apart by violence, repression, or migration; U.S.-based taxpayers unknowingly funding state terror abroad; Indigenous and Afro-descendant communities displaced by militarized development; as well as students, researchers, and civil society organizations exposing the global architecture of impunity. This tribunal does not simply ask *who pulled the trigger*, but *who built the gun, who paid for it, and who wrote the rules that guaranteed the shooter's escape.*

The 2009 Coup in Honduras: Manufactured Crisis, Managed Repression

On June 28, 2009, Honduran President Manuel Zelaya was forcibly removed from office in a military coup executed by U.S.-trained generals. Zelaya's "crime" was proposing a non-binding poll to gauge public support for convening a constituent assembly—a proposal that threatened elite interests and challenged the U,S.-imposed 1982 constitution. Within hours, Roberto Micheletti, the president of Congress, was installed as de facto president. The U.S. refrained from calling the event a coup and soon after began legitimizing

30 https://www.justice.gov/usao-sdny/pr/juan-orlando-hernandez-former-president-honduras-extradited-united-states-drug
31 See the appendix in this volume for more on the Permanent People's Tribunal.

the new regime.

The response from the Honduran people was immediate and massive. Protesters filled the streets, met by curfews, press blackouts, arbitrary detentions, and military repression. Over 4,000 people were detained in the first months of protest. The Inter-American Commission on Human Rights (IACHR) would later document widespread abuses: extrajudicial killings, torture, forced disappearances, and systematic violations of political rights.

Zelaya had implemented modest reforms—free education, a 60% wage hike, subsidies for the poor—and had begun aligning Honduras with ALBA and Petrocaribe, regional blocs independent of U.S. influence. His growing cooperation with Venezuela and other leftist governments drew the ire of Washington. In a 2019 interview, Zelaya recalled how U.S. officials—including John Negroponte and President George W. Bush—had warned him that relations with Chávez would "create problems with the United States." Six months later, he was exiled via Soto Cano Air Base, a U.S. military installation.

The parallels with previous U.S.-backed coups in Latin America were clear. The coup was orchestrated by generals trained at the U.S. Army School of the Americas. Ground and air operations were led by General Vásquez Velásquez (SOA '76, '84) and General Prince Suazo (SOA '96). The power grid was shut down during the operation—an old counterinsurgency tactic—ensuring media silence. Yet, despite this documented history and public condemnation from the UN and OAS, the U.S. under Secretary of State Hillary Clinton did not call for Zelaya's reinstatement. Instead, Clinton advocated for "order" and new elections—an approach that sidelined constitutional restoration and rewarded military intervention. A 2017 exposé of declassified documents published by The Intercept reveals that the U.S. Embassy's defense attaché, met with Honduran coup leader General Romeo Vasquez Velasquez the night before he led the 2009 coup that overthrew Manuel Zelaya.[32] The coup leaders who orchestrated Zelaya's ousting were U.S.-trained and held authoritative positions in military ground and air operations during the 2009 coup. General Romero Vásquez-Velásquez, a two-time U.S. Army School of the Americas

---

32 https://theintercept.com/2017/08/29/honduras-coup-us-defense-departmetnt-center-hemispheric-defense-studies-chds/ ; https://cepr.net/newsroom/investigation-reveals-new-details-of-us-role-in-2009-honduras-military-coup/ ; Frank, Dana, The Long Honduran Night, 19

graduate (1976, 1984) (today renamed "Western Hemisphere Institute for Security Cooperation"), served as the Chief of the Armed Forces of Honduras. Concurrently, General Luis Javier Prince-Suazo, a member of the SOA class of 1996, held the position of Chief of the Honduran Air Force during the 2009 coup.[33]

Post-Coup Changes:
"Honduras is Open For Business." Austerity to Narco-State

Following the contested 2009 elections, Porfirio "Pepe" Lobo, the first post-coup president, swiftly reversed the progressive trajectory Honduras had begun under Zelaya. Instead of defending public sovereignty, Lobo prioritized financial alignment with international institutions—the IMF, World Bank, and Inter-American Development Bank—securing billions in emergency loans while pledging structural reforms and austerity. A 2012 report from the Defense Technical Information Center (DTIC) of the U.S. Department of Defense noted approvingly that Lobo "quickly secured an emergency standby agreement with the IMF...as well as much-needed development financing," by agreeing to sweeping reforms.[34]

These IMF-backed reforms deepened the very inequalities that Zelaya's administration had sought to redress. Public sector wages were cut, subsidies slashed, and pensions de-indexed. The government enacted tax changes to increase revenue while offloading the cost of structural adjustment onto the country's most vulnerable. These measures—disguised as fiscal responsibility—reflected a broader political realignment: Honduras was being refashioned into a debt-dependent client of U.S.-led economic governance, its sovereignty bartered for financial liquidity. The post-coup regime—elected under highly contested conditions and marred by voter boycotts—ushered in an era of repression and impunity. NGO offices were raided, resistance leaders were murdered or exiled, and civil liberties were curtailed. Notably, the Committee of Relatives of Detained-Disappeared Persons (COFADEH) docu-

---

33 https://soaw.org/notorious-soa-graduates-from-honduras ; https://soaw.org/notorious-soa-graduates
34 See sources at: https://apps.dtic.mil/sti/citations/ADA584631 ; https://apps.dtic.mil/sti/pdfs/ADA584631.pdf

mented over 120 murders and at least 157 forced exiles between 2009 and 2010 alone. Despite these facts of repression, the U.S. praised the elections as a return to democratic order. The U.S.-backed regime of Porfirio Lobo (and later Juan Orlando Hernández, who rose through Congress post-coup) was positioned as a partner in "stability" and "reconciliation." The legitimization of the 2009 coup and subsequent elections laid the groundwork for a narco-state masquerading as a democracy—directly contributing to the mass displacement and political instability that persists today.

When Juan Orlando Hernández (JOH) assumed power in 2014, these trends accelerated. JOH further militarized the state, diverting resources from public education, health, and welfare into the security sector. His administration intensified surveillance, criminalized dissent, and deployed military-police hybrids against activists, journalists, and social movements. Under the pretext of fighting gangs and drugs, the state deepened repression—arming forces that, in many cases, operated with impunity and open political bias. Behind this militarized governance model stood an uncomfortable truth: the United States funded, armed, and legitimized the very security forces used to suppress Honduran civil society. U.S. taxpayers, many unaware of the destination of their dollars, financed weapons and training programs that sustained an anti-democratic regime and escalated human rights abuses.

By 2019, the cracks in the post-coup regime were no longer deniable. Juan Antonio "Tony" Hernández—JOH's brother and a former congressman—was convicted first in the U.S. for large-scale cocaine trafficking. In 2022, amid growing international scrutiny, JOH was extradited to the United States.

On March 8, 2024, a New York jury found him guilty of international drug trafficking and weapons charges. Only once JOH's crimes became indefensible, the U.S. distanced itself from JOH. Officials like Rubio, who had collaborated extensively with JOH, endorsing trade deals and security cooperation, became silent within a month. For years, the calls to end U.S. support of JOH's regime that were brought to DC by Hondurans and international advocates were ignored. Where was the retribution or even acknowledgment of wrongful delay? As the U.S. Congress failed to stop him, JOH's corrupt and repressive security apparatus had gone unchecked.[35] In a now scrubbed press release of a 2016 visit to Honduras, Marco Rubio stated:

> "A robust U.S.-Honduras partnership is now more important than ever," said Rubio. "In the past few years, we have worked together to confront security challenges affecting both America and Latin America. As a result, the country of Honduras has seen many positive changes, including a decline in violence. It is in our interest as a nation to continue to encourage a safe, prosperous Honduras with a thriving economy based on manufacturing, tourism, and agriculture. "I am particularly proud of the shared relationship and persistent trade between Florida and Honduras," Rubio continued. "I wish to continue strengthening this partnership as Florida ports and businesses work to collaborate on increased trading opportunities. Furthermore, the men and women of the U.S. military I encountered in Honduras are truly remarkable and essential to charting a prosperous future for this country. I look forward to continue improving U.S.-Honduras relations to maintain peace and stability in the hemisphere."[36]

Rubio's visit took place just four months after Indigenous land defender and critic of JOH's regime and U.S. intervention, Berta Cáceres, was assassinated in her home.[37] In addition to meeting with JOH during this visit, Rubio also met with the U.S.-trained National Police "Los Tigres," whose chief (El Tigre Bonilla) was implicated and found guilty for participating in JOH's narco trafficking regime.[38] U.S. officials, such as Marco Rubio, collaborated with JOH, endorsing trade and security deals while ignoring corruption. Today, the

35 For open support by Rubio see also: https://www.facebook.com/SenatorMarcoRubio/posts/met-with-president-juan-orlando-hernandez-and-foreign-minister-lara-of-honduras-/2165819073443445/;For reports on impunity that were introduced in congress see https://www.congress.gov/bill/117th-congress/house-bill/1574/text.

36 For access to the Wayback Machine press account of Rubio's 2016 visit with JOH, see: https://web.archive.org/web/20220827032954/https://www.rubio.senate.gov/public/index.cfm/2016/6/photo-release-rubio-concludes-official-trip-to-honduras

37 For an overview of the Berta Cáceres assassination that took place just before Rubio's visit in 2016. https://www.theguardian.com/world/2018/nov/29/berta-caceres-seven-men-convicted-conspiracy-murder-honduras

38 https://www.justice.gov/usao-sdny/pr/former-chief-honduran-national-police-charged-drug-trafficking-and-weapons-offenses ; https://www.cbsnews.com/news/ex-honduras-police-chief-the-tiger-sentenced-19-years-us-prison-cocaine-distribution/

history of Rubio's diplomatic visit to Honduras has disappeared from his official press release archives and internet pages. The aforementioned press release was accessed on the Internet Archive, which takes a snapshot of URL publications and web pages. If it weren't for the Wayback Machine Internet Archive resource, there would be no easily accessible proof of Rubio's visit or comments in support of JOH's regime during the period JOH was found to be trafficking drugs to the U.S.

This vicious double standard exemplified by Marco Rubio, points to what we learn in each successive generation: The U.S.-led War on Drugs is a narrative tool, a war on truth, justifying ongoing U.S. military and political interventions in Latin America in an anti-communist campaign of lawfare, just as the so-called war on drugs was a racialized campaign to criminalize and eliminate youth of color in the U.S. The state devises spectacular media campaigns comparable to the Central Park Five for its assault on individuals, communities, democratically elected leaders, and popular movements. Gang labels that were virtually nonexistent became living room sensations. Names like El Tren de Aragua or Cartel of the Sun have little to no bearing on reality in the state of Aragua, in Venezuela, or anywhere else. Yet, they were clearly fed to the specter of threat. Given its baseless absurdity, the 'criminal invasion' thesis has been repeated ad nauseam by the State Department. What is important to note is the thinness of the story, brazen in impunity.

The U.S. government's use of 'terrorist' designations is likewise meant to provide legal cover and justification for expanded U.S. militarization and interventions across Latin America, including in Honduras, Mexico, and Venezuela. In February 2025, the U.S. designated cartels as Foreign Terrorist Organizations (FTOs) and Specially Designated Global Terrorists (SDGTs). These designations move to: criminalize all material support, including financial aid of organizations identified; justify deportations and enhanced military measures to combat terrorist activities; pressure other nations to isolate targeted groups and heighten public awareness of identified "terrorist" organizations.[39] The designations of "terrorism" create the justification within the anti-immigrant policy agenda of the Trump administration to render

39 https://www.state.gov/designation-of-international-cartels ; https://www.state.gov/executive-order-13224

any person or group inadmissible into or deportable from the U.S. Moreover, they render the subject indefensible by law and predisposed to indefinite containment.

> In an August 2025 interview, Marco Rubio commented:
> "... Here's the thing: We cannot continue to just treat these guys as local street gangs. They have weaponry that looks like what terrorists, in some cases, armies, have. They control territory in many cases. Those cartels extend from the Maduro regime in Venezuela – which is not a legitimate government; we don't recognize the Maduro regime as legitimate.[40]

JOH's case reveals more than a singular instance of accidental corruption. The State Department projects its own image in guilt of complicity onto other sovereign nations, which serves to distract from the pattern of U.S. aggression that has only escalated through successive parties over decades. The U.S. weaponizes legal designations within the narratives of a counter-expansion to the War on Drugs and Terror, based on its own fabrications, to attack and assault in endless terror of its own.

In July of 2025, the U.S. Treasury Department released a press release accusing Maduro of heading a fictional organization called the Cartel of the Suns, designating it a terrorist entity. Rubio was quite explicit in initiating these absurd allegations to attempt military and surveillance invasion of Venezuela. None of his accusations bear any evidence. Trump then issued an order to the Pentagon authorizing military intervention in countries with drug trafficking.[41] As William Camacaro writes, "Washington demonstrates its contempt for the people of the Global South by treating their presidents as pawns, making accusations without any evidence, and imposing unilateral and illegal sanctions against those who resist imperial domination. This latest bizarre accusation should remind us of the allegations of the existence of weapons of mass destruction that served as an excuse to destroy Iraq, murder a million people, displace thousands from their homes, and deprive the nation of control over their natural resources" (2025).[42] An international tribunal on the damages of these actions would bear witness-

---

40   https://www.state.gov/releases/office-of-the-spokesperson/2025/08/secretary-of-state-marco-rubio-with-raymond-arroyo-of-ewtns-the-world-over
41   https://www.nytimes.com/2025/08/08/us/trump-military-drug-cartels.html
42   See William Camacaro, https://coha.org/washingtons-escalating-war-on-venezuela-narco-myths-and-imperial-designs/

es from the world to testify, from Los Angeles to Colombia where nearly half a million people were killed in the decades long so-called 'drug war' backed by the U.S. Plan Colombia.

In the meantime, pushback from Abya Yala is also growing with clarity of strategy and a vision of peace. In Honduras, Xiomara Castro was elected to office in 2021, Zelaya's wife and candidate with the leftist Libre Party, which was created as a political response to the coup. An alliance may be in the mix between Castro and Mexican President, Claudia Sheinbaum, who join leaders of the global South from Havana, Managua, La Paz, and Bogotá who are once again poised to reject the imperialist agenda.[43] After the U.S. announced an entirely illegal $50 million bounty for Maduro's arrest on the bogus charge of drug trafficking with Sinaloa cartels,[44] President Sheinbaum confirmed that no evidence was received, and rejected U.S. troops: "Mexico will not accept U.S. military forces in our territory," just as we say we will not accept the U.S. military forces in unjustified and illegal ICE attacks on our people in the streets of the global North.[45]

In sum, we judge complicity in JOH's crimes and call for a true reckoning for all people to examine the historical realities of U.S. imperialist intervention to piece together the broken stories across lands and time. Connecting the dots brings an imperative for true revolutionary change from within the U.S. Without it, the unchecked successive injuries allow the U.S. to target its victims over and over again in what amounts to systemic abuse, blaming them for seeking refuge, asylum, and survival from the perpetrator whether they are on one side of the border or the other.

Through its safeguarding measures, as the trial and conviction of Juan Orlando Hernández shows, the U.S. does not seek truth to reconcile. It systematically whitewashes its own hands of blood and blames instead its crimes onto the body of another. In this, recall the Doctrine of Discovery: "[...] we shall seize your possessions and harm you as much as we can as disobedient and resisting vassals. And we declare you guilty of resulting deaths and in-

43 https://www.usnews.com/news/world/articles/2025-08-08/mexico-has-no-evidence-linking-venezuelas-maduro-to-sinaloa-cartel-president-says https://www.yahoo.com/news/articles/mexico-no-evidence-linking-venezuela-235558119.html
44 See Camacaro 2025. For U.S. cooperation see: https://apnews.com/article/venezuela-fbi-bondi-justice-department-0e618369ca68b79b1a2143a95955344a
45 https://www.gob.mx/sre/prensa/statement-on-security-cooperation

juries, exempting Their Highnesses of such guilt as well as ourselves and the gentlemen who accompany us." Again, the thinness of U.S. justification, the directness and the patterns of these acts over history, and the impunity with which it operates lay bare the actual logic of U.S. imperialism. In the court of history, however, we know that the U.S. government is not an arbiter or judge—it is a complicit and guilty serial offender whose cover is cracking, and it will fall.

Works Cited

Amnesty International. "Honduras Failing to Tackle Coup Rights Abuses." June 28, 2010. https://www.amnesty.org/en/latest/press-release/2010/06/honduras-failing-tackle-coup-rights-abuses/.

Amnesty International. "Disappearances" in Honduras: A Wall of Silence and Indifference. London: Amnesty International, May 1992. https://www.amnesty.org/fr/wp-content/uploads/2021/06/amr370021992en.pdf.

Alterman, Eric. "Iran-Contra, the Sequel?" *Center for American Progress*, February 24, 2005, https://www.americanprogress.org/article/think-again-iran-contra-the-sequel/.

Cage, Jack H., et al. A History of Joint-Task Force Bravo. February 2020. https://www.jtfb.southcom.mil/Portals/14/documents/A%20History%20of%20JTF-Bravo.pdf.

Calderon, F. Garcia. "The Monroe Doctrine and Latin America." The Atlantic, May 28, 2022. https://www.theatlantic.com/magazine/archive/1914/03/the-monroe-doctrine-and-latin-america/645027/.

Camacaro, William. "Washington's escalating war on Venezuela: Narco-myths and imperial designs," Council on Hemispheric Affairs, Aug 12, 2025. https://coha.org/washingtons-escalating-war-on-venezuela-narco-myths-and-imperial-designs/

Campos, Rodolfo Pastor. "An Inconvenient Truth in Honduras." Foreign Policy in Focus, April 7, 2011. https://fpif.org/an_inconvenient_truth_in_honduras/.

Cano Contreras, Eréndira Juanita, Jaime T Page Pliego, and Erin I. J Estrada Lugo. "La Construcción de La Noción de Cosmovisión Maya En Guatemala." *Revista pueblos y fronteras digital* 13 (2018). https://doi.org/10.22201/cimsur.18704115e.2018.v13.336.

Caporaso, James A, and David P Levine. *Theories of Political Economy*. Cambridge; Cambridge University Press, 1992.

Center for Constitutional Rights. "Honduran Commission of Truth and CCR Launch Effort to Obtain Information from U.S. About 2009 Coup." March 24, 2011. https://ccrjustice.org/home/press-center/press-releases/honduran-commission-truth-and-ccr-launch-effort-obtain-information.

Center for Justice & Accountability. "Honduras." https://cja.org/where-we-work/honduras/.

Clinton, Hillary Rodham. *Hard Choices*. New York: Simon & Schuster Paperbacks, 2015.

Congressional Research Service, The Library of Congress. *Honduran-U.S. Relations*. Washington, DC: Congressional Research Service, July 25, 2012. https://apps.dtic.mil/sti/pdfs/ADA584631.pdf

Cochoy Alva, María Faviana, Pedro Celestino Yac Noj, Isabel Yaxón, Santiago Tzapinel Cush, María Rosenda Camey Huz, Daniel Domingo López, et al. *Cosmovision_Maya plenitud de la vida*. Ciudad de Guatemala: Programa de las Naciones Unidas para el Desarrollo. 2006.

Cohn, Gary, and Ginger Thompson. "When a Wave of Torture an Murder Staggered a Small U.S. Ally, Truth was a Casualty." *The Baltimore Sun*, June 11, 1995. https://webcitation.org/5j6KNYW6F.

Democracy Now. "Outsted Honduran President Zelaya: The 2009 U.S.-Backed Coup Helped Cause Today's Migrant Crisis." July 12, 2019. https://www.democracynow.org/2019/7/12/manuel_zelaya_honduras_coup_immigration_crisis.

Domingo Lopez, Daniel. *Q'anb'il qanq'ib'il, k'ujlab'il qchwinqlal. Sanar nuestra vida, amar nuestra vida en plenitud*. Ciudad de Guatemala: Fundación Centro de Documentacion e Investigacion Maya CEDIM. 2012.

Downy, Beau. "A History of Joint Task Force-Bravo." *Joint Task Force-Bravo*, April 7, 2020. https://www.jtfb.southcom.mil/Portals/14/documents/A%20History%20of%20JTF-Bravo.pdf?ver=2020-04-07-122737-510&timestamp=1586276868596.

EarthRights International. "Juana Doe et al. v. IFC." October 7, 2024. https://earthrights.org/case/juana-doe-et-al-v-ifc/.

Euraque, Dario A. "Cliché and Caricature." *Perspectives On History*, September 18, 2024. https://www.historians.org/perspectives-article/cliche-and-caricature-why-january-6-was-not-like-a-banana-republic-may-2021/.

Feller, Ben. "Analysis: Obama's Stand on the Honduran Coup." NBC News, June 30, 2009. https://www.nbcnews.com/id/wbna31669400.

Frank, Dana. *The Long Honduran Night: Resistance, Terror, and the United States in the Aftermath of the Coup.* Chicago: Haymarket Books, 2018.

Gilens, Martin, and Benjamin I. Page. "Testing Theories of American Politics: Elites, Interest Groups, and Average Citizens." Perspectives on Politics 12, no. 3 (2014): 564–81. https://doi.org/10.1017/S1537592714001595.

GovInfo. "Nomination of John Negroponte to Represent the U.S. at the United Nations." September 14, 2001. https://www.govinfo.gov/content/pkg/CREC-2001-09-14/html/CREC-2001-09-14-pt1-PgS9461-6.htm.

Gressier, Roman. *"La calidad de conversación con Arévalo depende de los pueblos indígenas."* El Faro, June 13, 2024. https://elfaro.net/es/202406/centroamerica/27458/la-calidad-de-conversacion-con-arevalo-depende-de-los-pueblos-indigenas.

Ham, Andrés. "Should developing countries increase their minimum wages?" World Bank Blogs, November 28, 2016. https://blogs.worldbank.org/impactevaluations/should-developing-countries-increase-their-minimum-wages-guest-post-andr-s-ham.

Han, Danielle. "Fruit Geopeelitics: America's Banana Republics." *JSTOR Daily*, April 9, 2023. https://daily.jstor.org/fruit-geopeelitics-americas-banana-republics/.

Haugaard, Lisa, and Sarah Kinosian. Honduras: A Government Failing to Protect Its People. Latin America Working Group Education Fund, March 2015. https://www.lawg.org/wp-content/uploads/storage/documents/Honduras-Failing-To-Protect-Its-People-Final.pdf.

Henry M. Jackson School of International Studies. "Theories of Political Economy." March 3, 2017. https://jsis.washington.edu/publication/theories-of-political-economy/.

Hernández, Juan Orlando (@JuanOrlandoH). "The success of Honduras was generated by the Honduran Attorney General, the police, the military, the courts, intelligence, ATIC, PMOP, working in cooperation together with the DEA, SOUTHCOM, State, DOJ, FBI, CIA, Treasury and DHS, to carry out our policy to battle the narcos." Twitter, February 3, 2022, 5:15 p.m. https://twitter.com/JuanOrlandoH/status/1489407288691634184?s=20.

Hove, Mark T. "The Arbenz Factor: Salvador Allende, U.S.-Chilean Relations, and the 1954 U.S. Intervention in Guatemala." *Diplomatic history* 31, no. 4 (2007): 623–663. https://doi.org/10.1111/j.1467-7709.2007.00656.x.

Isacson, Adam, Ana Lucia Verduzco, and Maureen Meyer. *Halfway to the U.S.: A Report from Honduras on Migration*. Washington, DC: Washington Office on Latin America (WOLA), June 2, 2023. 29 pp. Accessed via PDF. https://www.wola.org/wp-content/uploads/2023/06/2023-06_honduras_report.pdf

Johnson, Jake. "How Pentagon Officials May Have Encouraged a 2009 Coup in Honduras." *The Intercept*, August 29, 2017. https://theintercept.com/2017/08/29/honduras-coup-us-defense-departmetnt-center-hemispheric-defense-studies-chds.

Joyce, Rosemary A. "Legitimizing the Illegitimate: The Honduran Show Elections and the Challenge Ahead." *North American Congress on Latin America*, March 8, 2010. https://nacla.org/article/legitimizing-illegitimate-honduran-show-elections-and-challenge-ahead.

Main, Alexander. "Dirty Elections in Honduras, with Washington's Blessing." North American Congress on Latin America, January 11, 2018. https://nacla.org/news/2018/03/13/dirty-elections-honduras-washington%E2%80%99s-blessing.

Mérida Ponce, J. P., M. A. Hernández Calderón, O. Comandini, A. C. Rinaldi, and R. Flores Arzú. "Ethnomycological knowledge among Kaqchikel, Indigenous Maya People of Guatemalan Highlands." *Journal of Ethnobiology and Ethnomedicine* 15, no. 36. (July 17, 2019). https://doi.org/10.1186/s13002-019-0310-7.

National Security Archive. "The Iran-Contra Affair 20 Years On." November 24, 2006. https://nsarchive2.gwu.edu/NSAEBB/NSAEBB210/.

New York Times. "The Truth America Owes Honduras." October 9, 1995. https://www.nytimes.com/1995/10/09/opinion/the-truth-america-owes-honduras.html.

Office of the High Commissioner for Human Rights. "UN Declaration on the Rights of Indigenous Peoples." September 13, 2007. https://www.ohchr.org/en/indigenous-peoples/un-declaration-rights-indigenous-peoples.

Organization of American States. "Press Release R48-09." July 6, 2009. https://www.oas.org/en/iachr/expression/showarticle.asp?artID=754&lID=1.

Portillo, Suyapa, et al. "Honduras Holds Democracy Hostage." North American Congress on Latin America. December 12, 2017. https://nacla.org/news/2017/12/13/honduras-holds-democracy-hostage.

Prashad, Vijay. "Hyper-Imperialism." Consortium News, January 29, 2024. https://consortiumnews.com/2024/01/29/hyper-imperialism/.

School of the Americas Watch. "Notorious SOA Graduates from Honduras." March 6, 2019. https://soaw.org/notorious-soa-graduates-from-honduras.

Scott, Peter Dale and John Marshall. *Cocaine Politics: Drugs, Armies, and the CIA in Central America.* University of California Press, 1991.

Shakur, Shaka. "The New Modern Militarized Fort!," *Counterpunch*. Mar 2024.

Spring, Karen. "Day Twelve: JOH Finished Testifying & Court Heard Closing Remarks. The Trial Has Ended." Honduras Now, March 6, 2024. https://www.hondurasnow.org/day-twelve-joh-finished-testifying-court-heard-closing-remarks-the-trial-has-ended/.

Spring, Karen. "Narco-trial Update #9: Honduras Was 'Open For Business' (And Drug Trafficking)." Honduras Now. February 29, 2024. https://www.hondurasnow.org/narco-trial-update-9-honduras-was-open-for-business-and-drug-trafficking/.

Tricontinental. "Pity the Nation: Honduras is Being Eaten From Within and Without." April 12, 2021. https://thetricontinental.org/wp-content/uploads/2021/04/20210408_Dossier-39_EN_Web.pdf.

United Nations, Human Rights Council. *Anatomy of a Genocide: Report of the Special Rapporteur on the situation of human rights in the Palestinian territories occupied since 1967, Francesca Albanese.* March 25, 2024. https://www.ohchr.org/sites/default/files/documents/hrbodies/hrcouncil/sessions-regular/session55/advance-versions/a-hrc-55-73-auv.pdf.

U.S. Department of Defense. "Combatant Commands." https://www.defense.gov/About/combatant-commands/.

U.S. Department of Homeland Security. *Readout Of Secretary Kelly's Meeting With President Of Honduras Juan Orlando Hernandez.* March 22, 2017. https://www.dhs.gov/news/2017/03/22/readout-secretary-kelly-s-meeting-president-honduras-juan-orlando-hernandez.

U.S. Department of Justice. *Juan Orlando Hernandez, Former President Of Honduras, Convicted In Manhattan Federal Court Of Conspiring To Import Cocaine Into The United States And Related Firearms Offenses,* by Nicholas Biase and Lauren Scarff. Press Release Number: 24-089. March 8, 2024. https://www.justice.gov/usao-sdny/pr/juan-orlando-hernandez-former-president-honduras-convicted-manhattan-federal-court.

U.S. Department of Justice. *Juan Orlando Hernández, Former President of Honduras, Indicted on Drug-Trafficking and Firearms Charges, Extradited to the United States from Honduras.* Press Release Number: 22-411. April 21, 2022. https://www.justice.gov/opa/pr/juan-orlando-hern%C3%A1ndez-former-president-honduras-indicted-drug-trafficking.

U.S. Department of Justice. *Honduran National Geovanny Fuentes Ramirez Sentenced To Life In Prison And Ordered To Forfeit $151.7 Million For Distributing Tons Of Cocaine And Related Firearms Offenses,* by Nicholas Biase. Press Release Number: 22-036 February 8, 2022. https://www.justice.gov/usao-sdny/pr/honduran-national-geovanny-fuentes-ramirez-sentenced-life-prison-and-ordered-forfeit.

U.S. Department of State. *Assistant Secretary Brownfield's Travel to Honduras.* October 31, 2014. https://2009-2017.state.gov/r/pa/prs/ps/2014/10/233594.htm.

U.S. Department of State. *Honduras Election,* by Ian Kelly. Press Release Number: 2009/1185. November 29, 2009. https://2009-2017.state.gov/r/pa/prs/ps/2009/nov/132504.htm.

U.S. Department of State. *Reagan Doctrine, 1985.* January 20, 2009. https://2001-2009.state.gov/r/pa/ho/time/rd/17741.htm.

U.S. Drug Enforcement Administration. *Honduran Nationals Charged with Drug Trafficking Arrived in South Florida after being Extradited,* by Deanne L. Reuter. December 18, 2024. https://www.dea.gov/press-releases/2014/12/18/honduran-nationals-charged-drug-trafficking-arrived-south-florida-after.

U.S. Library of Congress. Congressional Research Services. *Honduran Politi-*

cal Crisis, June 2009-January 2010, by Peter J. Meyer. R41064. February 1, 2010. https://www.everycrsreport.com/reports/R41064.html.

U.S. Library of Congress. Congressional Research Service. *Honduras-U.S. Relations*, by Peter J. Meyer. RL34027. July 25, 2012. https://apps.dtic.mil/sti/citations/ADA584631.

U.S. Library of Congress. Congressional Research Service. *Venezuela: Overview of U.S. Sanctions*, by Clare Ribando Seelke. IF10715. August 8, 2023. https://crsreports.congress.gov/product/pdf/IF/IF10715.

U.S. Southern Command. "About Us." https://www.southcom.mil/about/.

U.S. Southern Command. "SOUTHCOM Commander Visits Central America, Discusses Regional Security Cooperation." January 25, 2019. https://www.southcom.mil/MEDIA/NEWS-ARTICLES/Article/1740966/southcom-commander-visits-central-america-discusses-regional-security-cooperati/.

White House. "Readout of Vice President Biden's Meeting with Honduran President Juan Orlando Hernandez." June 17, 2015. https://obamawhitehouse.archives.gov/the-press-office/2015/06/18/readout-vice-president-bidens-meeting-honduran-president-juan-orlando.

White House. "Remarks by President Obama After Meeting with Central American Presidents." July 25, 2014. https://obamawhitehouse.archives.gov/the-press-office/2014/07/25/remarks-president-obama-after-meeting-central-american-presidents.

Wright, Herbert. "The Bases of American Foreign Policy." *The Annals of the American Academy of Political and Social Science* 216 (1941): 99–108. http://www.jstor.org/stable/1023710.

Whitney, Jr., W. T. "Annals of Imperialism: U.S. Military Takes on Honduras." *Monthly Review Online*, June 2, 2012. https://mronline.org/2012/06/02/whitney020612-html/.

The Maya Dialectic Method: The Dialogues of Knowledge

Dr. Javier Mateos-Campos and Dr. B'eleje' Kan

In a recently discovered *Lost Interview* from 1971,[1] Michel Foucault questioned whether the universality of our scientific knowledge had been accomplished at the cost of exclusions, bans, and rejections as a kind of cruelty regarding reality. During this rare video interview, Foucault explained that the legitimization of Western scientific thinking as the standard of truth came at the expense of the negation, marginalization, exploitation, and erasure of other worldviews and paradigms, including the cultural genocide of Indigenous ways of knowing. As Foucault brilliantly put it, "We suppressed madness, and as a result, we came to know it; we suppressed foreign cultures, and as a result, we came to know them." At the dawn of coloniality in the Americas, negation, exclusion, and suppression became the acceptable means through which the West understood and justified the destruction of Indigenous people(s) and their cultures. Once the brutal military campaigns were over, European concerns centered on cultural domination via Christianization to dispossess Indigenous people of their culture, history, and language to subjugate them spiritually and materially as a strategy to prevent rebellions and armed uprisings (Cintli Rodríguez, 2014).

Nevertheless, successive generations of Maya people in America, *Abya Yala*, have safeguarded a legacy of ancestral knowledge from the destruction, theft, and cultural genocide they have endured for centuries (Cochoy Alva et al., 2006). According to Fray Bartolomé de las Casas, one of the first friars who documented Maya writing, the Spanish colonizers burned hundreds of Maya books (Christenson, 2007). Upon the destruction and banishment of

---

1 *Foucault, The Lost Interview*. From Dutch Tv in 1971, conducted by Fons Elders in preparation for his debate with Noam Chomsky. https://youtu.be/qzoOhhh4a-Jg?si=0m19Z6jaLrZsecAf

most written sources, the Maya people codified their ancestral knowledge in ingenious ways of cultural resistance, such as memorizing oral tradition or weaving intricate textile patterns with hidden meanings (Campos-Navarro, 2023). To this day, Western academics have a limited understanding of the rich Maya Kosmovision[2] and an even more rudimentary comprehension of the extensive oral tradition and dialectic practices of the Maya Kaqchikel people who have inhabited the highlands of Guatemala and its surrounding territories for millennia (Mérida Ponce et al., 2019).

Guatemala has a long history of oppression and death by American imperialism. The coup orchestrated by Washington against the socialist government of Jacobo Arbenz in 1954 spiraled the country into decades of brutal, CIA-backed military dictatorships that inflicted systemic violence against Maya populations (Hove, 2020). In 2023, the political alliance between the Indigenous-led WINAQ party and the progressive SEMILLA party closed ranks behind their candidate, Bernardo Arévalo, and won the presidential race by a landslide. Despite a frustrated coup attempt, President Arévalo took office in 2024 thanks to the Maya leadership mass mobilizing the WINAQ-SEMILLA political bases, which paralyzed the country for days. His presidency has generated hope and expectation for the thousands who rallied behind him to take firm steps toward a genuine democratic transformation of public life in Guatemala. After centuries of colonial neglect, the future of Guatemala can no longer be envisioned without including the revolutionary Maya people and their ancestral knowledge(s) from the street level to the highest echelons of government decision-making. The Maya Kosmovision has a fundamental role to play in the construction of a democratic future for the people in Guatemala and the hundreds of thousands of Maya migrant workers living permanently or temporarily in the United States.

The Maya Dialectic Method is integral to the rich Maya Kosmovision and Maya Kaqchikel oral tradition. Also known as the Dialogues of Knowledge (DofK), these are formal dialogue circles with multiple uses, including ped-

2   Kosmovision written with a "K" represents resistance. According to the Maya oral tradition, this is the original way Maya scribes during the colonial period wrote it. It was the friars who changed its written form to "C" in their letters back to the Spanish crown. We write it with a "K" to honor the labor of many Maya people and their cultural resistance against erasure and domination.

agogical practices, community organizing, conflict resolution, cultural diffusion, and political purposes, to name a few. The Dialogues of Knowledge are a democratizing praxis that has been strategic for knowledge sharing, community healing, governance decisions, collective organizing, and preserving oral traditions across generations. With the recent democratic transition in Guatemala, Indigenous people have entered all sectors of government in record numbers, bringing with them their oral tradition and dialectical practices. The Dialogues of Knowledge are an essential part of these cultural practices and have quickly become key democratic strategies in the governance process of the newly elected government[3].

The Maya Kosmovision and the Dialogues of Knowledge

The Maya Kosmovision emanates from a scientific-spiritual paradigm based on natural cycles and mathematical principles that mark exact calendars, interpret the qualities of the days, and give testimony to a profound human connection with the universe (Cochoy Alva et al., 2006; Contreras et al., 2018). The Maya Kosmovision represents a knowledge system based on a deep mathematical understanding of the Earth's natural cycles. This means that it produces mathematically accurate and profoundly spiritual knowledge precisely because it is rooted in the interconnectedness of the Cosmos and human consciousness (Domingo-Lopez, 2012). For example, the methodical observance of corn's harvesting cycles, which best aligned with the rotation of the Moon, gifted the Maya people with a concise understanding of time rooted in the movement of the Earth and the Cosmos (Domingo-Lopez, 2012). Developing incredibly accurate cyclical calendars that described the spiritual qualities of the days (Cochoy Alva et al., 2006). This starkly contrasts with Western modern thinking, which has confined spirituality exclusively to religion or limited approaches from academic disciplines like psychology or cultural anthropology. In other words, Western science and highly capitalistic societies are deeply deprived of a profound sense of spirituality that involves a reciprocal connection with Earth, which continues to dehumanize our existence (Marker, 2011).

---

3 Reporting by Gessier, 2024. https://elfaro.net/es/202406/centroamerica/27458/la-calidad-de-conversacion-con-arevalo-depende-de-los-pueblos-indigenas

According to the *Popol Vuh* (1947), the sacred book of the Maya, the Gods Tepeu and Gucumatz had the first dialogue of creation that sparked human consciousness and manifested the material world. This sacred narrative explains that nothing existed at the beginning of time, only the sea and the sky in the darkness of the night. The spoken word of the first dialogue between Tepeu and Gucumatz brought light and clarity to their thoughts and words. Interestingly, the *Popol Vuh* situates the Dialogues at the very beginning of the development of human consciousness, characterizing the spoken word as a humanizing condition. With each dialogue circle, the Dialogues of Knowledge honor the first dialogue between the Maya Gods that gave rise to humanity. Maya oral tradition indicates that ever since, the Dialogues have provided an emerging perspective for the profound codification of life and its movements that recognize intuition and critical thinking as trailblazers in the search for the meaning of life (Cochoy Alva et al., 2006).

The DofK are formal dialogue circles in which participants follow a specific protocol that assigns them a chronological order to talk in designated rounds. As a synergizing principle in the Dialogues, no individual truth is privileged over another but interwoven in emerging patterns of meaning and representation. The Dialogues appeal to our capacity to learn differently through the transformative power of language and storytelling as participants share their reflections and connect them with the realities expressed by others. The main idea is to interweave your life experience with the shared reflections of other participants in a meaningful and cohesive way. The Dialogues seek to create a meeting point, a temporal interruption of the linearity of everyday life, to entice radical openness for participants to see their humanity in their experiences and those of others. The Dialogues move in a humanizing and collaborative motion that seeks a deeper understanding of social and material reality to ultimately transform it.

In highly capitalist societies, human interactions have become increasingly transactional in an economic system that dominates most people's time (Hardt & Negri, 2001). Capitalism's atrocious influence on social relations has gradually destroyed meaningful community relations to the point of alienating people even from themselves[4]. Engagement with the Dialogues seeks to go beyond the transactional nature of modern everyday life by allowing participants to sit in a circle, tune in, listen, and synthesize in reciprocity with others. An activity that is rarely prioritized within the time limitations in most people's daily lives. In this sense, the Dialogues of Knowledge underpin a humanizing space to reclaim our capacity to (re)connect with one another in an increasingly dehumanizing and alienating modern world. The next part provides an illustrated explanation of the protocols guiding the Dialogues, accompanied by an example that serves as a point of departure for engaging with the DofK.

Engaging with the Dialogues of Knowledge

WA'IX / ZERO

The Maya Kosmovision is based on a scientific-spiritual paradigm that has ancestrally accumulated mathematical knowledge about Earth's natural cycles and the Universe (Cochoy-Alva, 2006). The Cosmos is recognized as the source of all knowledge, which provides the Maya Kosmovision with an incredibly accurate and profoundly spiritual dimension. A non-existent condition of thought in Western modern knowledge that objectifies nature and disregards spirituality as lacking any scientific value, often categorizing it like folklore or antiquated beliefs from the past. Instead, the Dialogues are Maya science with its strong mathematical connections with the Earth applied dialectically in the social world. For the Maya Kosmovision, recognizing each other's humanity through dialogue constitutes a spiritual experience.

The Dialogues assign a Maya number chronologically to each person representing the participation sequence, starting with Zero (Wa'ix), who

4 Katya Colmenares, 2024. Pensar lo Gravísimo y Reconstruir el Tejido Comunitario. YouTube https://youtu.be/vD0K_Rl2gy4?si=C6B_UesWctutsmJj

serves as moderator. Zero (Wa'ix) is the first person to speak and present the protocol. One (Jun) is the second person, two (Ka'i') is the third person, and three (Oxi') is the fourth person. They all followed the same underlying principle: "The human role is to participate in the orderly design of nature" (Kawagley and Barnhardt, 1998, p.4). Zero lays out the initial *threads* or themes to construct in the Dialogues. This person is also in charge of opening and closing the circle. Zero opens the Dialogues with the following words from the *Popol Vuh* (1947), the sacred book of the Maya People:

> This is the relation of how all was in suspense, calm and silent, and motionless, in a quiet and empty extension of the sky. This is the first relation; these were the first words. Back when there was not yet one person, animal, bird, fish, crab, tree, rock, hollow, canyon, meadow, or forest. Only the Sky exists all alone. The face of the Earth had not yet appeared. Alone lies the expanse of the sea. All alone, the Sky exists. Nothing was gathered together yet that would make noise, not even something that would move or make noise in the Sky. There was not yet anything standing erect. Only the infinite expanse of Water, only the tranquil sea lies alone.
>
> There was not yet anything that might exist. Only immobility and silence in the darkness of the night lay placid and silent in the darkness, in the night. Only the creator and formator in the darkness of the night, the progenitors Tepeu and Gucumatz, were in the water surrounded by light. They were under green and blue feathers. That is why they were called Tepeu and Gucumatz. They were wise, great thinkers; it was in their nature . . . The spoken word arrived, and they joined in the darkness, in the night, and talked to each other, consulting and meditating; they agreed and joined their words and thoughts. Then appeared clarity while they meditated.

Figure 1: Tepeu and Gucumatz sitting on space and time (Lopez, 2023)

The person representing Zero (Wa'ix) will then present the following protocol, which will guide the movement of the Dialogues of Knowledge (DofK):

- You will receive a number for your turn to speak.
  Order synergizes the form and creates dialogue.
- Wait for your turn to speak.
  Space and time form and create dialogue.
- There is no hierarchy or oppressive binaries. All voices are equal.
  Intertwine your voice and knowledge with the experiences of others.
- Focus and reflect on your personal and collective experiences first.
  Engage in constant reflection; listen, reflect, and weave in your experience.
- Active Attention.
  Weave your experiences with the emerging themes of the dialogues.
- Consensus as a source of knowledge.
  A Place and Time for Re-visions and Wisdom.

It is important to note that consensus in the Dialogues does not necessarily mean one general agreement or accord among the experiences of all participants. Absolute truths are of no interest to the Dialogues. The consensus represents the last round of individual participation, reflecting on the most meaningful themes, elements, and reflections from the Dialogues. The consensus is a tapestry of multiple individual contributions.

The Dialogues involve disrupting the transactional nature of human relations in the modern world through a series of relatively easy-to-follow steps. Not to be reductionist, but its genius resides in its simplicity. Spatial theorist Edward Soja (1996) explained that it is not easy to understand and accept everyday life as the primary site of capitalist exploitation, domination, and struggle, where alienation and mystification of human consciousness occur. Capitalism has forever transformed all human relations and social interactions (Hardt & Negri, 2001). The Dialogues aim to disrupt the alienation and transactional rhythm of everyday life by opening up a space that allows people to recognize their humanity by seeing themselves reflected in the experiences of others—a temporal alternative to the disconnection with one another that is present in most modern daily social interactions. The Dialogues serve as a humanizing force that momentarily creates a new geography, a new frequency for social interactions to engage in dialogue on an entirely different wavelength of action by listening, reflecting, and weaving in their experiences with those of others in an ongoing dialogue.

And the dialogues will continue...

Zero as the Cosmic Seed in the Spiral of Wisdom

Ideally, participants will sit around a table (although not mandatory), and each will be assigned a number representing the order of participation. One must not speak out of turn. The order is intentionally directed to create a dialectic synergy among participants. Breaking the sequence means also breaking the circle. The Maya Dialectic Method can be visualized as a moving circle or in the sacred form of a spiral. With each round of participation, the themes in the dialogue increase in intensity, complexity, and depth. The Dialogues can have two or more participation rounds depending on time constraints and the number of participants. We recommend at least two rounds so that everyone can participate at least twice, but one round of full participation is also possible for larger groups with limited time.

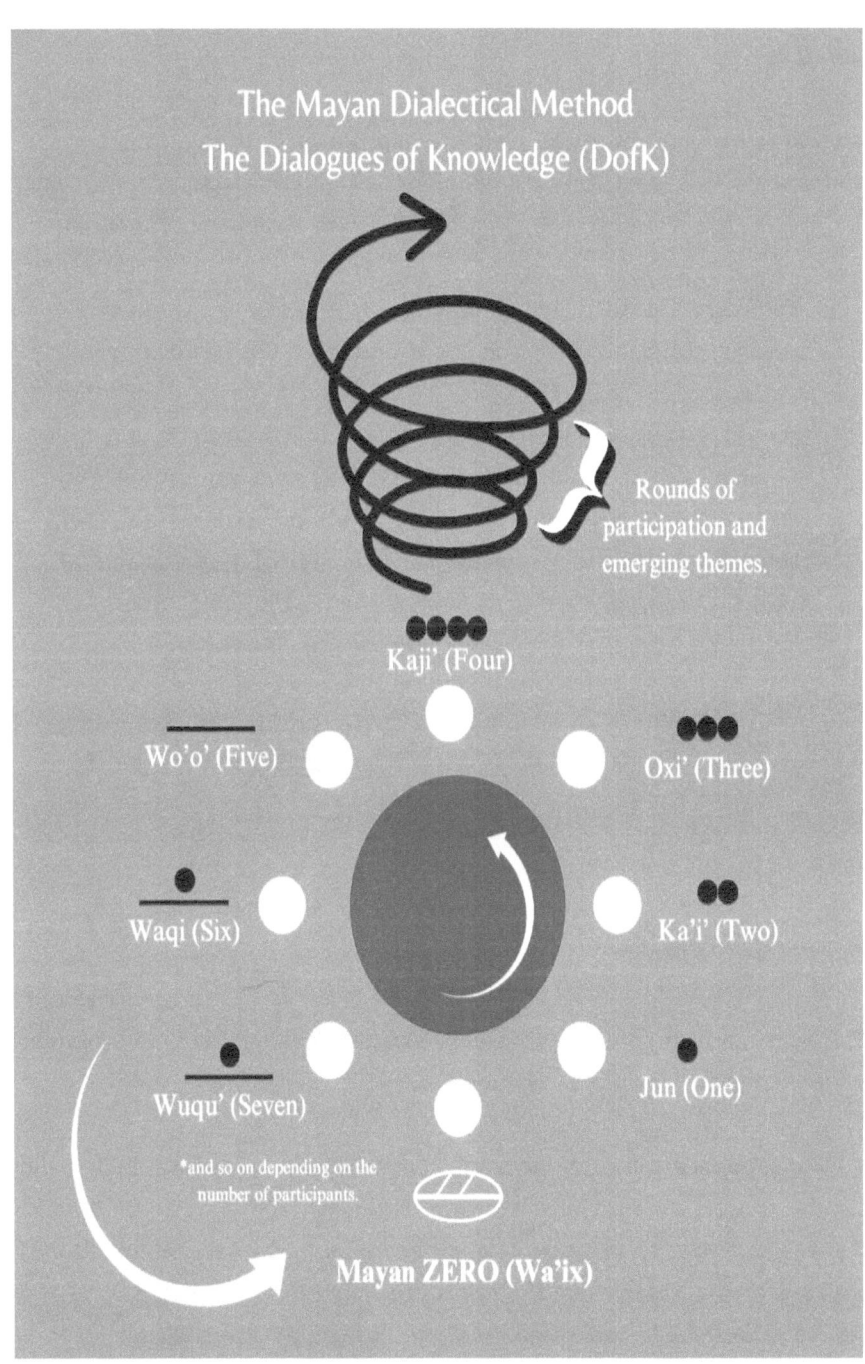

Figure 2. The Maya Dialectical Framework

Jun (One)

After Zero has presented the structure and protocols of the DofK, the second person, who represents the number one (Jun), introduces the following words from the sacred text *Popol Vuh* (1947), which represent Jun (one):

> "Then came his word, and together, the Heart of Sky arrived with the sovereign Quetzal Serpent in the darkness, in the night. He spoke with sovereign Quetzal Serpent. They talked together, and then they thought, and they pondered. They reached an accord, bringing together their words and their thoughts. They gave birth, heartening one another. Beneath the light, they gave birth to humanity. Then they arranged for the germination and creation of the trees and the bushes, the germination of all life and creation, in the darkness and the night, by the Heart of the Sky" (*Popol Vuh*, 1947)

Ka'i' (Two)

The third person, in turn, represents Ka'i' or number two and continues with the protocol and the DofK.

Oxi' (Three)

The fourth person, in turn, represents Oxi' or number three, and continues with the protocol and the Dialogues.

The sequence will continue until all participants speak for a first round and the process then will revert to Zero for the next round. Zero (Wa'ix) asks if participants wish to engage in another round for however many rounds they feel are necessary. Zero then closes the circle by doing a consensus as a source of knowledge and a place and time of (re)visions and wisdom.

According to Maya oral tradition, closing words are necessary to end the Dialogues of Knowledge. We recommend the following closing words:

"I am closing the circle, and all energies will stay in this circle and elevate in a spiral to the Sky where the Maya Gods will observe humanity following their first dialogue in the Universe."

K'amöl B'ey, Dialectic Synergy and The Sacred Spiral

In the Mayan Kaqchikel language, one interpretation of the term *K'amöl B'ey* (pronounced Kamul Béq) refers to someone who carries, brings, and takes knowledge to guide themselves and others. In the Dialogues of Knowledge, all participants are equal K'amöl B'ey. Each participant embodies a K'amöl B'ey, bringing and taking knowledge while recognizing each other as valuable knowledge holders. The Dialogues have a performance or ceremonial component, but this does not mean the content participants express is scripted or acted out. On the contrary, participants' shared experiences flow organically, and the multiplicity of associations connecting them is entirely unpredictable. Each K'amöl B'ey is a fragment of the dialogue circle, which, after multiple rounds of participation, can be better visualized as fragments of a sacred spiral.

Due to its profound mathematical understanding of nature, sacred geometry plays a fundamental role in developing Maya knowledge. In the Maya Kosmovision, the spiral is part of the sacred geometrical patterns that are consistently present in living beings' biological patterns. It is well-known that biological beings demonstrate remarkable repeatable patterns governed by mathematical laws and regularities, which frequently exhibit symmetry (Bormashenko, 2022). Historically, mathematicians from Greek, Hindu, and Muslim civilizations studied sacred geometry in search of a golden ratio or divine proportion. The golden ratio refers to a correlation of numbers that occurs in the growing pattern of natural dynamic systems (Omotehinwa, 2013). Popularized in the West by mathematician Leonardo Fibonacci during the Middle Ages, the spiral, in particular, has illustrated the mythical golden ratio present in the life-sustaining structures of multiple living beings such as plants, flowers, the reproduction of rabbits and bees, and even in the human hand (Omotehinwa, 2013). The spiral is a pattern in nature that is known for its self-similarity, meaning it grows and develops in size without changing shape or by maintaining the same shape (Omotehinwa, 2013).

For Maya mathematicians, sacred geometry is nothing new, as they have long studied and accumulated knowledge about numerical correlations and ratios present in nature. Captivatingly, the concept of self-similarity of the spiral also explains the intention of the Dialogues for participants to see their humanity reflected in each other by sharing and weaving their life experiences in the circle. Through the Dialogues of Knowledge, the Maya Kosmovision applies mathematical principles to establish a dialectical format guided by the natural patterns and ratios that synergize the Earth. The structure of the Dialogues mirrors the organic flow of symmetrical patterns that emanate from nature dialectically through the shape of a spiral. By following the circular/spiral pattern of participation, the Dialogues seek to set in motion a dialectic synergy that offers a symmetrical modality on how we relate to one another, rooted in correlation and reciprocity. Each K'amöl B'ey attentively gives and takes knowledge accordingly to maintain the dialectical synergy in cohesive motion.

Dialogues of Knowledge in Practice

The following explanation includes the participation of four people in a dialogue circle that took place in Sonoma, California to exemplify the Dialogues of Knowledge. The dialogue circle took place during the fall of 2024 and included four participants identifying as educators, activists, and community organizers who are actively involved in social justice and transformative work. The Dialogue centered on their experiences as educators and social activists and how those experiences inform an educational vision for the future. The purpose of this example is to explain the steps and protocols and illustrate the weaving of emerging themes in a meaningful tapestry of representation.

The following Spiral of Wisdom (see Figure 4) visualizes some of the words or threads spoken during the dialogue circle in Sonoma. It is important to note that the fragments are intentionally not expressed in a strictly linear structure but arranged in spiral form as smaller fragments of wisdom that can be read sequentially or individually. The order follows the chronological order of participation, starting with Wa'ix or Zero, the Cosmic Seed at the center of the Spiral of Wisdom.

Contemplation, Tapestry of Knowledge (Fragments of the Spiral of Wisdom)

The final consensus or *tapestry of knowledge* emerges once all participants in the dialogue circle have completed their final round of participation.
Again, in the DofK, consensus does not mean one final agreement or determination but the plural inclusion of the final thoughts of all participants.
The written representation of the tapestry of knowledge intentionally breaks

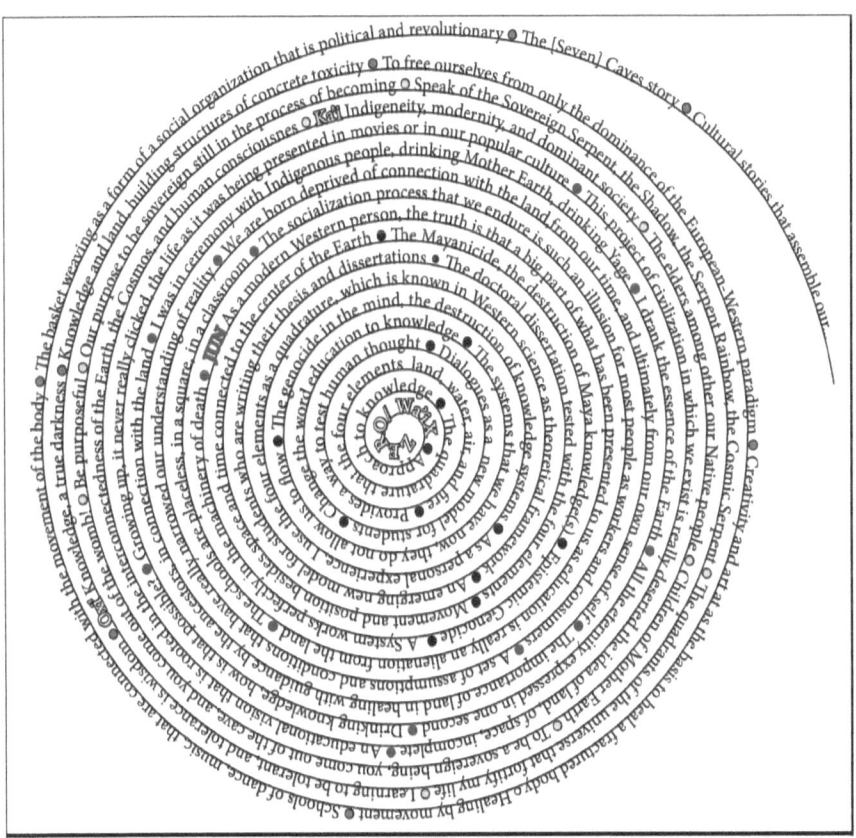

*Figure 4. The Sacred Spiral of Wisdom that emerged from the Dialogue at
the Center for People Power in Aguas Calientes (Tso-noma), California*

away from a strict academic format that demands narrow structures and interpretations of knowledge. Instead, the tapestry is read more freely, allowing readers to insert their own perspectives in interpreting the text.

Within the spiral of wisdom, the DofK proposes a guiding quadrature or *quadrant* constituted by the four sacred elements of nature (Air, Fire, Earth, and Water). This quadrant serves as a frame of reference for examining emerging themes from a dialogue circle. The examination serves as a reflexive praxis to ensure that the work being done prioritizes a connection with the Earth through the principles of self-determination, self-identification, sovereignty, and autonomy for participants and Indigenous people(s). In the Maya Kosmovision, the presence of the four sacred elements in the Dialogues should ultimately generate social actions rooted in such principles for the community. Although the Maya Kosmovision rejects the term *"theoretical framework,"* this concept is the closest to the notion of the Maya quadrature in Western social sciences.

The following is the tapestry of knowledge that emerged from the dialogue circle in Sonoma (Tso-noma), after passing it through the quadrature of the four elements. The text is meant to be read as individual fragments of the Spiral of Wisdom expressed by participants in their final participation round.

Wa'ix' (Zero)

In the Maya Kosmovision, the power and value of words are essential for understanding the Maya approach to knowledge.

The quadrature, including the four elements of Air, Fire, Earth, and Water, provides a frame of reference to examine human thought concerning the Earth and the Cosmos.

The pedagogical goal of the Dialogues is to provide an alternative for students to move away from traditional *education* models and instead engage with *knowledge* creation.

This system allows a flow of knowledge that transcends the limitations of institutionalized education.

Maya cultures continue to face the destruction of their sacred ways of knowing, the dispossession of the lands, and the loss of their traditional ways of living.

Maya elders emphasize the importance of contemplation as a way to revise one's inner self and understand the principles, ethics, and values that guide our worldview.

Only deep reflection and contemplation can lead to a profound understanding of the natural synergy that interconnects all beings with beautiful, sacred geometry. In times of darkness, finding safety in Mother Earth's womb, symbolized by zero, provides a sense of security and grounding in the face of the adversity that imperialism poses in every step of humans searching for life balance.

Jun (One)

The idea of home and connection to a specific place is important in Indigenous cultures, whereas in Western societies, the concept of home has become more concrete and connected to physical locations.

Against the modern domination of time keeps us busy and empty, with barely enough air to breathe,

Home is close to the heart,

A life made up of love momentums.

In the midst of the flow of economic systems and a focus on controlling and exploiting natural resources, everything is engulfed in despair and death.

Dialogues to (re)humanize the time and space that is our life.

Ka'i' (Two)

The universal quadrants fortify my life, continually learning how to be tolerant, and tolerance is wisdom.

The Serpent, the Shadow, the Serpent Rainbow, and the Cosmic Serpent symbolize the interconnectedness of all things and the need to fortify life with knowledge and wisdom. I have a cousin who took 15 years to finish his doctorate. The institution destroyed him. Indigenous peoples encounter academic institutions that do not always value or respect their ways of knowing.

I'm tired of hearing that we are privileged people. We're not privileged.

We're deeply spiritually deprived of our connection to each other and with Mother Earth.

The dismantling of traditional family structures and the loss of traditional trading routes, which were taught to us by the animals, highlight the urgent need for a concrete educational vision that reclaims and revitalizes Indigenous ways of being and knowing.

America's like a movie, full of realities on how to exist in an imperialist system.

Oxi' (Three)

Creativity to heal a fractured body; there's healing and truth in movement.

We need schools of dance, music, theater, and other disciplines that connect students closer to the performance arts.

Indigenous communities transmit knowledge and values through narrative and symbolism. Learning involves moving through space and time. Indigenous practices like basket weaving serve as artistic expressions, forms of social organization, and political resistance.

Basket weaving is a metaphor for a fierce, inclusive, political, and intensely revolutionary form of social organization.

A vision for a pluricultural education.

Considerations for the Future in the Dialogues of Knowledge

The cultural legacy of centuries of colonization imposed an ever-increasing form of social decomposition through a web of extreme individualism, arrogance, and insatiable greed that transformed humans into profoundly materialistic individuals with consumption-oriented lifestyles that go against the multiple forms of life that coexist in the Universe (Cochoy Alva et al., 2006). Prophetically, Maya ancestors visualized and predicted these times when humans destroyed nature for profit, naively thinking of themselves as the owners of everything. At the same time, the avarice of a few marginalized and oppressed the vast majority of the population from basic rights - they called it *El No Tiempo* (Cochoy Alva et al., 2006).

According to the Maya cyclical conception of time, *El No Tiempo* does not represent an apocalyptic end of times but a transitional period of social renovation aligned with the movement of the Cosmos. The Maya Kosmovision proposes the Dialogues as an important dialectical tool to strategize and politically activate the community during these unprecedented times of planetary crisis for humanity. The Dialogues offer a democratizing praxis to (re) Indigenize the future in a capitalist world that has increasingly become more unequal and authoritarian. A dialectic renovation that underpins a counterweight to modern alienation through an inclusive, participatory vision that prioritizes life and community over profit and individualism. The following section includes three areas of promise for the future of the Dialogues of Knowledge.

The Dialogues as Democratic Praxis

Guatemala is currently undergoing a historical democratic process. The conservative right-wing sectors that have traditionally held political power were defeated in the recent election, and the promising beginning of Arévalo's left-leaning Presidency is evident. However, right-wing sectors still hold huge economic influence in the country and exert significant power in Congress. A coalition of Indigenous groups led by the WINAQ party has proven to be a decisive political ally for President Arévalo. On the other hand, this coalition is also a highly organized social movement ready to paralyze the country if the newly elected government fails to fulfill its political commitments. The political atmosphere in Guatemala is tense, as a right-wing coalition in Congress continues to disrupt negotiations at the Dialogue tables and block the much-needed key reforms for the country[5]. In contrast, the Dialogues have gained success and popularity in urban and rural locations across the country in diverse modalities that go from improvised street dialogue tables in public areas to formal dialogue circles of resolution between Indigenous authorities and government officials.

The Dialogues as democratic praxis have encountered a historical momentum to push back against more than 500 years of colonial domination in Guatemala. The Maya people have joined Dialogue tables across the territory

5   Guatemala Congress News *Congreso imprueba estado de calamidad* [Congress News]. Congreso de Guatemala. https://www.congreso.gob.gt/noticias_con-greso/11671/2024/4#gsc.tab=0

in unprecedented numbers to organize and regain community control of local government structures. The DofK has operationalized collective organizing to pursue concrete objectives such as winning local elections, cleaning political parties of corruption, or rejecting mining and oil companies from sacred territories. The Dialogues show promise as a democratizing tool and participatory strategy to regain political power from a small white elite that has enriched itself through centuries of colonial exploitation in a country where more than 40% of the population identifies as Maya (INE, 2019).

The Dialogues to Indigenize The Resistance

According to Maya oral tradition, the Dialogues of Knowledge have always played a fundamental role in Indigenous people's struggle for land, sovereignty, autonomy, self-determination, and self-identification (Domingo Lopez, 2012). Indigenous communities continue to face huge risks of further destitution of their lands, natural resources, culture, language, and traditional practices. Some of the main concerns of Maya leaders who seek inclusivity in President Arévalo's national project involve Indigenous land and the protection of sacred territories against concessions made by the previous government to transnational oil, mining, and logging companies (CONAPO, 2023). The Dialogues have emerged as an important organizing tool and resistance strategy in the pushback against transnational companies and the efforts to obtain legal protection for sacred territories. In these cases, the Dialogues have ensured that the Maya leaders and government resolutions prioritize Mother Earth and the principles of sovereignty, autonomy, self-determination, and self-identification for the Indigenous people of Guatemala.

The political crisis in the country during 2023, which started with an attempted coup by a right-wing coalition, sparked mass mobilizations and the implementation of improvised dialogue tables in urban and rural settings. Maya Kaqchikel, Mam, Quiche, and Tuztzujil leaders, among others, joined in a national uprising that halted the country. The resistance against the coup was fierce, and the Dialogues kept people informed and energized for several days. The mass mobilization of Maya groups defied the government and took over strategic highways and other pieces of critical infrastructure, including access to the national airport in Guatemala City. Incorporating the Maya Kosmovision through the Dialogues as organizing and knowledge-sharing strategies in diverse acts of resistance generated a unique momentum that got Maya leaders closer to dissatisfied communities, some of which had previously failed to organize politically. The people's response to the Dialogues was unprecedented precisely because the DofK offered a space of cultural communion and concrete lines of action to channel popular frustration against the rampant corruption attempting to steal the election.

The Dialogues of Knowledge quickly became instrumental in organizing and pursuing the takeover of political power under a Maya leadership structure. More important than the takeover of power by the Maya groups in active resistance is setting the conditions for new forms to exercise the circulation and orientation of state power in more equitable and life-sustaining ways. The conditions are set for the Maya people to Indigenize the resistance and new governmental practices of power. Amid this democratic transition, Maya leaders used the wisdom of the Popol Vuh (1947) to find clarity and guide the movement through the current political landscape with the following words: *que nadie se quede atras* (no one left behind)!

The Dialogues as Pedagogy and Methodology

As mentioned earlier, the Maya Kosmovision emanates from a scientific-spiritual paradigm with a deep mathematical understanding of the Earth's natural cycles and their connections to human consciousness. A fundamental aspect of the Dialogues involves the expansion of consciousness through learning, particularly about ourselves and our relations to others. The Dialogues have been incorporated in classrooms and other learning spaces to incentivize respectful exchange of experiences and ideas among students and professors. As a pedagogical practice, the Dialogues offer a non-hierarchical model in which students recognize themselves and others as valuable knowledge holders. The Dialogues of Knowledge can be incorporated as a dialectical tool in the curriculum where students learn about themselves, their relations with others, and the complexities of the world around them. Particularly for students from minoritized backgrounds, finding academic spaces that speak to their lived experiences becomes a lifeline for navigating college.

Research has shown that students who consistently see themselves reflected in the coursework are less likely to drop out and have higher retention and graduation rates (Doran, 2022).

The intense political momentum that has set in motion a democratic transformation in Guatemala has echoed in other areas of public life. In recent years, higher education in Guatemala has witnessed the rise of educational initiatives from diverse Maya groups to establish their respective Houses of Knowledge to preserve, research, and diffuse Maya knowledge. The Universidad Maya Mam, Universidad Maya Kaqchikel, and Universidad Ixil are examples of these initiatives that are leading an authentic Maya cultural and scientific revival. One of the most interesting trends in these newly formed universities is the proposal to adopt the Dialogues of Knowledge instead of the conventional interviews that dominate qualitative research in the social sciences. The Dialogues as a research methodology must be rooted in one or more of the four pillars of social cohesiveness for the Maya people: self-determination and self-identification against cultural domination, sovereignty over their land and laws, and autonomy to keep the movement rooted in the community.

The Dialogues have also been utilized as strategies to fortify research teams by strengthening bonds among researchers while providing a space to share and theorize different perspectives. Moreover, the Dialogues also expand the available repertoire of research tools for the social sciences in disciplines such as Ethnic Studies or other humanities that involve research in partnership with Indigenous and other vulnerable populations. Strikingly, the word *research* does not exist in the Mayan Kaqchikel lexicon. Instead, the Mayan Kosmovison proposes *community service* as the pedagogical arena where personal, familiar, and communal experiences coalesce for the expansion and maturity of human consciousness (Cochoy Alva et al., 2006). *Nimajay*, *La Casa Grande*, or Big House (or house of the community) is the closest translation in the Maya Kaqchikel vocabulary for the word university, revealing the community's central position in the construction of knowledge. Community service constitutes the base of recognition, authority, and political power that maintains social cohesion and a shared sense of kinship among the Mayan Kaqchickel people. In other words, for Maya science, learning about the community involves working and serving within the community and not doing extractive research on them or of them, as is often the case in the Western social sciences.

Works Cited

Barnhardt, R., & Oscar Kawagley, A. (2005). Indigenous knowledge systems and Alaska native ways of knowing. *Anthropology & Education Quarterly*, *36*(1), 8–23. https://doi.org/10.1525/aeq.2005.36.1.008

Campos-Navarro, R., Dorantes, L., & Cavaleri, D. D. (2023). Los bordados mayas que protegen de enfermedades en el estado de Yucatán, México. *Segundo Congreso Internacional de Iconografía Precolombina. Barcelona, 2023. Actas.*

Cano Contreras, E. J., Page Pliego, J. T., Estrada Lugo, E. I. J., Cano Contreras, E. J., Page Pliego, J. T., & Estrada Lugo, E. I. J. (2018). La construcción de la noción de Cosmovisión Maya en Guatemala. *Revista pueblos y fronteras digital*, *13*. https://doi.org/10.22201/cimsur.18704115e.2018.v13.336

Christenson, Allen J. *Popol Vuh : The Sacred Book of the Maya* Norman: University of Oklahoma Press, 2007.

Claris, Lionel. *Foucault–The Lost Interview*. Lionel Claris. March 20, 2014. YouTube video, 15:46. https://youtu.be/qzoOhhh4aJg.

Cochoy Alva, M. F., Yac Noj, P. C., Yaxon, I., Tzapinel Cush, S., Camey Huz, M. R., Lopez, D. D., Yac Noj, J. A., & Tamup Canil, C. A. (2006). *Cosmovision_Maya plenitud de la vida.* (First Edition). Programa de las Naciones Unidas para el Desarrollo.

Consejo Nacional de Areas Protegidas. (2015). *Plan maestro reserva de la biosfera. Segunda actualizacion* (p. 316) [Technical Document].

Domingo López, D. (2012). *Q'anb'il qanq'ib'il, k'ujlab'il qchwinqlal. Sanar nuestra vida, amar nuestra vida en plenitud*. Fundación Centro de Documentacion e Investigacion Maya CEDIM.

Doran, E. (2022). 'A space for beginning': Teaching Mexican American studies in Texas community colleges. *Race Ethnicity and Education*, *0*(0), 1–20. https://doi.org/10.1080/13613324.2022.2047637

Hardt, M., & Negri, A. (2001). *Empire* (First Edition). Harvard University Press.

Hove, M. T. (2007). The Arbenz factor: Salvador Allende, U.S.-Chilean relations, and the 1954 U.S. intervention in Guatemala*. *Diplomatic History*, *31*(4), 623–663. https://doi.org/10.1111/j.1467-7709.2007.00656.x

Instituto Nacional Estadistica Guatemala. (2019). *Resultados censo 2018* (p. 378) [Census]. INE.

Mérida Ponce, J. P., Hernández Calderón, M. A., Comandini, O., Rinaldi, A. C., & Flores Arzú, R. (2019). Ethnomycological knowledge among Kaqchikel, indigenous Maya people of Guatemalan Highlands. *Journal of Ethnobiology and Ethnomedicine*, *15*(1), 36. https://doi.org/10.1186/s13002-019-0310-7

Recinos, A. (1950). *Popol Vuh: The sacred book of the Quiché Maya people.* University of Oklahoma Press.

Rodríguez Cintli, Roberto. (2014). *Our Sacred Maíz Is Our Mother: Indigeneity and belonging in the Americas*. Tucson: University of Arizona Press, 2014. https://muse.jhu.edu/pub/208/monograph/book/34900.

Soja, Edward W. *Thirdspace Journeys to Los Angeles and Other Real-and-Imagined Places*. Cambridge: Blackwell, 1966.

Conclusion:
Principles and Pasos for a Zone of Peace

During the writing of this book, the White House has continued to escalate its attacks against our family and neighbors of the South under the pretense of the age-old and disproven propaganda of the 'war on drugs' and 'criminal' migration. As we go to press, warships are positioned off the coast of Venezuela, reminding us of the Niña, the Pinta, and the María, but in hyperbole form with missiles and thousands of trained soldiers. Such acts by the current direct assaults, kidnappings, and killings, systematic crimes against humanity, both within and outside of the U.S. borders bring Americanism into closer view, a violence repeated by imperialist continuity over centuries.

From 1492 to the present, the criminalization of survivors, of travelers, of labor and Earth is but a continuation of anti-Indigenous genocidal policies of the state, including closures of the border, to the mass deportations under the Clinton-Obama administrations, to the present-day vicious attacks by ICE raids. Exemplified by the ongoing U.S. official denial and continued arming of the genocide against the Palestinian people underscores U.S. military complicity in producing state-sanctioned crimes against humanity and then attempting to conceal the reality of such a crime from public memory.

People's Tribunals are vital in resisting this erasure by for-profit, racist, crusader systems operating today. Participants and witnesses take into account their own community response of actions and responsibilities. They also allow us to more fully expose the complicity within our institutions in order to ultimately end genocide once and for all. The shipping and weapons industry, including surveillance technology, is the private sector of the U.S. government's war machine. Component parts that are built in our university laboratories must be audited for their role in genocide. We deserve this transparency as members of the university community to know what our institution is doing in our name and with our bodies for its name. Without such transparency, we are forced into a non-consensual relationship that subverts our knowledge, our labor, our identities, and the very purpose of our lives.

The essays of this book present a range of tribunals from formal, ceremonial events with a beginning, middle, and end, to a specific kind of critique that is organized around historical accountability. To tribunalize is a new kind of scholarship, one that bends towards the form of a manifesto, and acts as an indictment. In both, the People's Tribunals find their power in long strides to make sense of a story of time but with direct intervention to repression. In this sense, the 500-year-plus struggle is to gather up time in order to adequately characterize and make sense of the scale of criminality caused by specific institutions, organizations, persons and offices as much as systems.

Usually these crimes follow predictable patterns of abuse. But the question of tribunals should always be asked, who is adjudicating, what is the evidence, who will enforce the verdicts, and what of the accused? Is it a people's court as gimmick or mere instrument of power, or is it a mechanism by the oppressed or the colonized to decolonize? What we have gathered in this book draws on the legacy of past tribunals to share with future movements for truth-telling and resistance. We have described the tribunal as a movement building process, a framework for critique, and a method to create political assembly. In all, the People's Tribunal provides essential space for testimony, collective organizing, and information in multiple forms to clearly see truth, and through it to reinforce the principled arguments and practice of building popular power.

With this aim, we share the following principles for the development of assemblies towards a bio-regional zone of peace:

- **Asserting our earthly right for mobility with no harm**

Mobility is a sacred and ancestral right, predating colonial borders and rooted in relationships with land, water, and kinship. Today, that right is criminalized—weaponized through surveillance, militarized borders, and forced displacement. True mobility without harm affirms the right to migrate, organize, and return with dignity—on terms defined by the people themselves.

- **Ending the settler colonial project**

In the April 2024 report entitled "Anatomy of a Genocide," UN Human Rights Rappoteur, Francesca Albanese, describes genocide as "inherent to settler colonialism" with the understanding that "genocide is a process, not an act [...] [r]anging from physical elimination to the 'forced disintegration,' of a people's political and social institutions, culture, language, national sentiments, and religion." The report cites settler colonial aims to acquire Indigenous land and resources. "Settler-colonialism," the report says, "is a dynamic, structural process and a confluence of acts aimed at displacing and eliminating Indigenous groups, of which genocidal extermination/annihilation represents the peak" (UN 2024). Ending the settler project is a clear imperative.

- **Land back, name back, free the land**

Land back with Indigenous Traditional Ecological Knowledge leadership is the basis for liberation. These practices are restorative of native plants and knowledge systems of fire and cultural burns, reseeding, and water flow. In this process, we recognize street names, cities and towns, building names, shops and businesses that do not deserve to carry the names of serial killers, rapists, or racists. We support land back, and amplify the prerogative to free the land to support liberated zones in the north as much as the south.

- **Ensuring an informed participatory judicial process**

New modalities for popular power include assemblies, dialogue circles, caravans, speaking tours, and the People's senate.[1] By popular power, we refer to the practice of establishing power outside of a representational system, towards direct democracy. This means centering the voices of those most impacted through grassroots assemblies, dialogues, and collective decision-making. The Tribunal is an active support system for these modalities, including repurposing theaters, streets, and public plazas as spaces for community forums and assembly. Popular power is the collective equivalent of organized mutual aid realized within a neighborhood, a region, as a people.

1 See the Spirit of Mandela at spiritofmandela.org for more information on organizing a People's Senate.

- **Commit to upholding the enshrined rights of Indigenous peoples**

The United Nations Declaration on the Rights of Indigenous Peoples (UN-DRIP) is an international instrument adopted by the United Nations in 2007. It enshrines the rights for the survival, dignity, and well-being of Indigenous peoples worldwide. The Declaration covers human rights related to Indigenous peoples, including self-determination, participation in decision-making, respect for culture, and equality. This process is guided by protocols including the principle of Free, Prior and Informed Consent (FPIC) for Indigenous Peoples, Native Nations, and First Nations, as affirmed by international law, which guarantees their rights to approve or reject actions that impact their lands, cultures, and lives.[2]

- **Generate a South-North cross-border alliance**

Engage in a practice of envisioning a South-North alignment with abolitionist principles leading the Caribbean-Pacific as a zone of peace in the hemisphere. Recognizing that Ayti (Haiti) is ground zero of the invasion, and sustains its struggle in the present day. Whereas many nations of the Global South need us to stop U.S. imperialism from the inside, North-South alliances deepen the work of 500 Years of Resistance. Taino ancestors Hatuey and Anacoana, followed by Victoria Montou 'Gran Toya" and Dessalines, were leaders of the continental liberation of the Americas, the hemispheric lands known by the Kuna people as Abya Yala.

- **Amplify the organizing efforts of incarcerated movement leaders**

Many of our strongest movement leaders have endured an unjust judicial and incarceration system. We stand firmly in the denunciation of prisoner abuse, including forced and prolonged isolation, torture, the removal and tampering with personal items, censoring education materials, and preventing barriers to personal growth, access to family, and health care. The barbaric illogics of the Prison Industrial Complex is an extension of slavery and must be abolished. Free all political prisoners now!

2 https://www.un.org/development/desa/indigenouspeoples/publications/2016/10/free-prior-and-informed-consent-an-indigenous-peoples-right-and-a-good-practice-for-local-communities-fao/

- **Making community access to education in community**

Political participation begins with access to popular education and the ability to share knowledge across generations. Without access to true information and the capacity to learn together in our communities, we can not engage with informed consent. We need our own media networks and centers for community education in every neighborhood to learn from each other in all areas of life, including in health, histories, arts and sciences.

- **Continue to build mutual aid**

Charity performs generosity while reinforcing hierarchies between giver and receiver; mutual aid emerges from horizontal relationships and a shared recognition that we keep each other alive, offering alternatives to the bureaucratic and depoliticized logic of charity under capitalism. Rooted in ancestral, intergenerational traditions of Indigenous, Black, migrant, and working-class communities, mutual aid is a reciprocal practice of care, survival, and resistance. It builds autonomy, trust, and political consciousness while centering the values of reciprocity, interdependence, community-driven care and the redistribution of production and resources in our daily lives. Mutual aid includes: bartering, skill sharing, seed exchanges, collective childcare, community clinics, kitchens and gardens, political education, and rapid response networks—practices that reject commodified care and refuse to rely on institutions that cause harm. It is not only how we survive, but how we build the conditions for liberation, together.

- **Support the Tribunals**

People's Tribunals disarm the violence of denial. An assertion of sovereignty through the tribunal allows participants to name, to choose, to unite in struggles. They are forums to educate, to learn, to be heard. These are spaces to speak truth and create specific measures for accountability in the collection and documentation of evidence. It is a pedagogy, a process, and a method that holds meaning, tradition, and innovation. The effects of tyranny bear significant impact and implications, with the Tribunal as one way to overcome, to find justice, and restore balance.

Appendix: People's Tribunal Reference Summaries

Originally compiled by Dayani Albuquerque

The following appendix provides a limited selection of tribunals and major campaigns generated from various people's movements around the world as a reference for further research.

1. Abya Yala Original Justice Tribunal
2. Bolivia's Talantaña Proposal for Planetary Harmony
3. Caribbean & Africa's Proposed International Tribunal
4. Commission for Historical Clarification (CEH)
5. FOSPA Tribunal
6. Global Tribunal on Palestine
7. International People's Tribunal on U.S. Imperialism
8. International Tribunal in Vieques
9. Mexico's Tren Maya Project
10. Peace Summit 2023
11. People's Permanent Tribunal
12. People's Tribunal Against Rep. Eric Swalwell
13. Popular Tribunal About Ferrogrão Project
14. Russell Tribunal on Palestine
15. Second Russell Tribunal on Latin America
16. Spirit of Mandela International Tribunal
17. Taxpayers Against Genocide
18. The Hague Group
19. The International Rights of Nature Tribunal
20. The Special Jurisdiction for Peace (JPE)
21. The UC People's Tribunal for Palestine
22. Tribunal Unitário Agrário (TUA) (Unitary Agrarian Tribunal)
23. The International Tribunal for Democracy in Brazil
24. Women's International War Crimes Tribunal on Japan's Military Sexual Slavery

1   Abya Yala Original Justice Tribunal
Peru | 2012-

The Abya Yala Original Justice Tribunal (Tribunal Originario Abya Yala de Jus-
ticia, TOAJ) was established in response to the mandates from the United
Nations, particularly following the directives of the 11th Session of the UN
Permanent Forum in 2012. This tribunal was tasked with addressing the historical grievances and systemic injustices perpetrated against Indigenous
Peoples by colonial states for over 500 years. It aimed to condemn these
states and secure reparations for the damage caused by acts of genocide,
ecocide, and the usurpation of Indigenous lands and rights. One of its significant actions was to issue sentences against three main entities based on
claims from the indigenous nation of Pacajes: the Spanish Crown, for its historical role in colonizing the Americas; the Vatican, calling for the abolition of
the Papal Bulls that legitimized the donation of Indigenous lands to colonizers; and the Bolivian state, for denying autonomy to the Pakajaqi ancestral
nation. Moreover, the tribunal advanced a maritime claim on behalf of the
Qullana Aymara people. This claim asserted their sovereignty over territorial
seas contested between Peru and Chile, thereby challenging the historical
and ongoing impacts of colonial and state policies on Indigenous territories
and rights. The Abya Yala Original Justice Tribunal saw participation from various indigenous councils, justice amautas (wise persons or teachers) from
ayllus (community family units), markas (sectors or divisions), and suyus (regions) from both highlands and lowlands. Additionally, the tribunal focused
on the historical context provided by the UN's directive for recognizing and
compensating Indigenous Peoples for the damages caused by colonial states
over the last 500 years. The first sentence issued by the tribunal, which addressed reparations from the Spanish Crown, the Vatican, and Bolivia for
their respective roles in the historical injustices suffered by Indigenous Peoples, was a significant material outcome of the tribunal's establishment and
proceedings.

2   Bolivia's Talantaña Proposal for Planetary Harmony
Bolivia | 2024

The Talantaña Proposal for Planetary Harmony in Tiwanaku, Bolivia, convened a diverse assembly of Indigenous peoples, scientific experts, state authorities, and entrepreneurs, united in their dedication to fostering planetary harmony. This gathering was focused on integrating ancient wisdom with contemporary scientific insights to navigate the challenges of climate change and promote the well-being of the planet. Participants spanned a broad spectrum, including Indigenous leaders, academics committed to environmental and Indigenous issues, and representatives from various organizations committed to ecological and cultural preservation. This diverse assembly underscored the importance of collective action and cross-cultural dialogue in addressing global environmental challenges. The outcomes of the tribunal were encapsulated in the ABYA YALA RESOLUTION, emphasizing the critical need for a synergistic approach between ancestral wisdom and modern science. The resolution included the declaration of Mother Earth as a subject of rights and the promotion of master plants for their healing properties, signaling a commitment to integrating traditional knowledge in the pursuit of ecological balance and sustainability. The tribunal also produced significant material, including the comprehensive resolution document outlining commitments to environmental stewardship, cultural preservation, and the promotion of traditional medicine and knowledge.

3   Caribbean and Africa's Proposed International Tribunal
Jamaica, Ghana, Nigeria, South Africa | 2022-

The tribunal is envisaged as a judicial mechanism similar to ad-hoc courts like the Nuremberg trials, aimed at addressing crimes related to enslavement, apartheid, genocide, and colonialism. It seeks to establish legal norms for handling complex international and historical reparations claims. In other words, this proposed tribunal aims to address historical atrocities related to the transatlantic slave trade, with support building among African and Caribbean nations. Key participants in pushing for the tribunal include African and Caribbean nations, specifically the African Union (AU) and the Caribbean Community (CARICOM). Notably, individuals like Eric Phillips, vice-chair of the CARICOM reparations commission, and Martin Okumu-Masiga, Secretary-General of the Africa Judges and Jurists Forum (AJJF), have been instrumental. Additionally, the United States has shown support through backing a UN panel central to this effort. The proposal was formally recommended by the UN Permanent Forum on People of African Descent and discussed at a summit in Ghana. The goal is to establish a tribunal through the United Nations system that involved discussions with countries historically linked to the slave trade such as Portugal, Britain, France, and others.

4   Commission for Historical Clarification (CEH)
Guatemala | 1997-1999

The Commission for Historical Clarification was established in 1994 to address massive human rights violations committed by the Guatemalan government and U.S. -backed paramilitaries against Mayan communities in which over 200,000 people were killed (83% Mayan and 17% Ladino). The Commission was created after the UN brokered peace agreement of 1996, 'to foster tolerance and preserve the memory of the victims.' The commission operated under a two-year mandate and employed three commissioners who found that repressive practices were perpetrated by institutions within the state, in particular the judiciary. The report stated that in the four regions most affected by the violence, "agents of the state committed acts of genocide against groups of Mayan people" (Final Report, English Version, para. 122). In total, it is reported that they conducted 7,200 interviews with 11,000 persons, including declassified information from the U.S. government. The document notes, "state forces and related paramilitary groups were responsible for 93% of the violations documented" (Final Report, English Version, para. 15), wherein "Insurgent actions produced 3% of the human rights violations and acts of violence" (Final Report, English Version, para. 21).

copadeh.gob.gt/guatemala-memoria-del-silencio

5   FOSPA Tribunal
Bolivia | 2002-

Violations of the rights of Indigenous women from the Amazon and the Andes were reported in this tribunal held during the XI Pan-Amazonian Social Forum (FOSPA) in Rurrenabaque, Bolivia. The situation of the Wayoró women was reported by the chief Walda Wajuru in a video testimony. Walda was supposed to speak in person at the tribunal, but she was prevented from boarding the flight to Rurrenabaque, a victim of a discriminatory act by the airline Latam. In her speech, she denounced human rights violations in the Wayoró Territory, in Alta Floresta D'Oeste, Rondônia, and the physical, sexual, and spiritual aggression against Wayoró women, who lead the fight for land defense. The FOSPA tribunal recommended that the Brazilian State implement policies to ensure recognition of the Wayoró territory; guarantee access to justice for indigenous women who are victims of gender-based violence; respect free, prior, and informed consultation regarding initiatives that impact indigenous territories; and sanction private companies and individuals responsible for violations in the Wayoró Territory.

forosocialpanamazonico.com

6   Global Tribunal on Palestine
Geneva | 2024-

The Global Tribunal on Palestine (GTP), held in June 2024 in Geneva, aimed not only to document the crimes of the state of Israel, and present them before the world in order to prosecute their perpetrators, but also to contribute to efforts being made to prevent the recurrence of such crimes. The means to do this will be through an impartial international judiciary that adheres to universal human rights principles and international standards of justice and integrity. This civil society initiative is being organized jointly by five Geneva-based human rights NGOs: the Scandinavian Institute for Human Rights FHM-Geneva; the International Union of Jurists – Geneva; One Justice; the Geneva Centre for Democracy and Human Rights; and the International Institute for Peace, Justice and Human Rights. The initiative is endorsed by the Global Legal Alliance for Palestine including major officials and more than 20 professors of international criminal law, doctors, journalists, and jurists who worked in Gaza with lived experience to illuminate truth about what has happened to their colleagues in terms of killings, arrests, and torture. One of their central objectives is to enable universal jurisdictions and immediate trial for perpetrators of war crimes among other demands.

7   International People's Tribunal on U.S. Imperialism: Sanctions, Blockades, and Economic Coercive Measures

Multiple Locations | 2023-

The International People's Tribunal on U.S. Imperialism: Sanctions, Blockades, and Economic Coercive Measures was an initiative aimed at building systems of accountability to challenge the impact of U.S. sanctions through a legal framework and cross-movement solidarity. In U.S. terminology, 'sanctions' are often framed as a form of non-violent discipline to rogue nations. Yet U.S. government agencies frequently deploy sanctions against otherwise democratically elected governments to force regime change with extraordinarily violent results including mass famine, destruction to health infrastructure, economic sabotage of some of the world's most impoverished communities, and the root cause of mass migration. Organizers held hearings on the impact of sanctions in 16 countries of the world, primarily the Global South, representing Cuba, Ethiopia, Eritrea, Haiti, Iran, Iraq, Lebanon, Libya, Palestine, Nicaragua, North Korea, Sudan, Syria, Venezuela, Yemen, and Zimbabwe. Expert witnesses from each location were heard. Organizers add that, "The countries chosen are not exhaustive of states impacted by U.S. sanctions but are emblematic of the role and function of imperialist sanctions as well as the multiple levels and forms of impact." A publication was made accessible with the findings in multiple languages. Materials created as part of the tribunal's efforts included comprehensive reports from special rapporteurs and the final verdict issued at the closing event. These materials are pivotal for the continuation of efforts to challenge sanctions and economic coercive measures imposed by the U.S.

internationalpeopletribunal.wordpress.com

8   International Tribunal in Vieques
Puerto Rico | 2000

The International Tribunal in Vieques condemns the U.S. Navy's violations of human, water, and land rights in Vieques, Puerto Rico. The Committee for Human Rights in Puerto Rico, under the direction of Dr. Luis Nieves Falcón and the Committee for the Rescue and Development of Vieques (CRDV) sponsored and organized the Tribunal. For several years, the CRDV coordinated visits by international delegations for demilitarization and decontamination, along with the Fellowship of Reconciliation and the Caribbean Project for Peace and Justice. The Tribunal denounced U.S. Navy violations internationally, recognizing that they result from the colonial condition of Puerto Rico, the repression against those who fight for Independence, and the presence of the U.S. Navy on Vieques. The participation of judges from Asia, Africa, America, and Europe contributed to the international dissemination of information about the Vieques case. Several ex-political prisoners of Puerto Rico also participated in the Tribunal.

9   Mexico's Tren Maya
Yucatán | 2023

The Tren Maya project in Mexico was initiated by former President Andrés Manuel López Obrador in September 2018 and one year later it became part of the larger National development plan. The tribunal on the Tren Maya Project centered on examining the ecological damage and cultural impacts caused by the construction of the Tren Maya railway. This railway project, spanning five Mexican states, has been under scrutiny for its potential to cause significant ecological destruction and for not respecting the rights of indigenous peoples. Indigenous communities directly affected by the Tren Maya, along with environmental specialists, brought forth their concerns to a distinguished panel of judges. These judges, renowned for their expertise worldwide, were tasked with assessing the project's impact from the Rights of Nature perspectives. The outcomes of the tribunal were significant, with the judges ruling that the Tren Maya project constituted acts of ecocide and ethnocide. This groundbreaking verdict demanded an immediate halt to the construction activities on the Yucatán Peninsula and called for the demilitarization of indigenous territories affected by the project. The tribunal's decision underscored the severe ecological damages and cultural infringements imposed by the Tren Maya, prompting a reevaluation of the project's sustainability and ethical foundations. By articulating the ecological and cultural impacts of the Tren Maya, the tribunal has contributed to the global discourse on sustainable development and the protection of vulnerable ecosystems and communities.

10   Peace Summit
Mexico City | 2023

The Peace Summit focused on addressing critical issues such as gun violence, migration, inequality, and climate change that affect communities across borders. This summit aimed to foster a shared strategy for tackling these multi-layered challenges by bringing together various stakeholders for meaningful dialogue and action. The event was organized by Global Exchange and saw the participation of over 300 community leaders and civil society organizations from multiple regions, including Mexico, the U.S., Colombia, Honduras, Haiti, and Canada. It served as a platform for victims of violence, Indigenous Peoples, migrants, and Black communities to share their stories and struggles and to strategize together against discrimination, violence, injustice, poverty, environmental devastation, and inequality. The summit yielded a variety of outcomes including the development of a binational agenda that emphasized the prioritization of human rights, stopping the illegal flow of weapons, demilitarization, respect for migrants' rights, and recognition of systemic racism, among others. These priorities are part of a broader effort to create a peaceful and just future for communities impacted by these issues. More than 50 partner human rights organizations, activists, and communities of color committed to working together to advance this shared vision of peace and justice for the region. The summit's collaborative approach highlighted the interconnectedness of the destinies of the U.S. and Mexico and their movements for social and environmental justice.

globalexchange.org/peace-summit-2023

11   Permanent Peoples Tribunal
Multiple Locations | 1979-

The Permanent People's Tribunal is an independent international institution based in Rome, and operating globally to recognize complaints against governments or private parties for violations of the rights of peoples. The panel of judges in each session are usually comprised of human rights lawyers and advocates who hear testimony of victims, witnesses, historians, and other affected parties and experts. As an antecedent of the Bertrand Russell Tribunals, sessions of the PPT have been heard since their founding in 1979, now exceeding 50 sessions, most notably against mining industries and transnational environmental crimes and other crimes against humanity committed for example, by Jair Bolsonaro, the Canadian Mining Industry, and actors in complicity with genocide in the Gaza Tribunal in Sarajevo. The PPT was founded by Lelio Basso who initiated the Universal Declaration of the Rights of Peoples adopted by the UN in Algiers on July 4th, 1976, declaring in the first four articles that every people has the right to existence, respect, return to territory, and that "[n]one shall be subjected [...] to massacre, torture, persecution, deportation, expulsion or living conditions such as may compromise the identity or integrity of the people to which [they] belong." The articles continue to outline the right to political self-determination; economic rights of peoples; right to culture; right to environment and common resources; rights of minorities; guarantees and sanctions. The last article (30) reads, "The re-establishment of the fundamental rights of peoples, when they are seriously disregarded, is a duty incumbent upon all members of the international community." The Permanent Peoples' Tribunal on Missing Indigenous Children and Unmarked Graves created a platform for global scrutiny committed in the failure of the Canadian legal system with public sessions beginning in 2026. See our-truths.com.

permanentpeoplestribunal.org

12   People's Tribunal Against Rep Eric Swalwell
East Bay, California | 2024

The People's Tribunal against Rep. Eric Swalwell was organized by East Bay 4 Ceasefire Now, a diverse coalition aiming to pressure locally elected representatives to end what they describe as the Palestinian genocide. This historic event took place on March 30th, where over 100 citizens found Swalwell guilty of complicity in the Palestinian genocide and failure to represent his constituency, marking the first time a People's Tribunal in the U.S. has held a member of Congress individually accountable for genocide. This sets both an ethical and political precedent that is applicable to other members of Congress and elected officials. These organizations and individuals came together to hold Swalwell accountable for actions and failures to act, which they argue have aided and abetted ongoing genocide in Gaza and Palestine through various forms of support. The trial was based on the principles of the UN Genocide Convention and federal laws against genocide, reflecting a broader movement to hold officials accountable at an international level. Testimony and arguments from key witnesses and members of the prosecution team were presented, alongside a detailed audiovisual and documentary record based on Swalwell's public statements and legislative activities.

eastbay4ceasefire.org/tribunal

13 Popular Tribunal: Ferrogrão in the Defendant's Chair[1]
Santarém, Pará, Brazil | 2020

Representatives of Indigenous peoples, traditional communities, organizations, and social movements from Pará and Mato Grosso held a People's Tribunal on March 4, 2024, to judge the impacts of the Ferrogrão project. This project intended to build a 1,000 km railway through the heart of the Amazon, proposed by the transnational companies Cargill, Bunge, Louis Dreyfus, and Amaggi to the Federal Government of Brazil. The Tribunal was composed of organizations and indigenous communities, representatives of fishing communities, family farmers, and social movements who determined the immediate and definitive cancellation of the Ferrogrão project by the Federal Government, holding the above mentioned companies of accountable for the damage caused to nature and the inhabitants of the Tapajós and Xingu regions. This decision was based on serious planning flaws, violations of the rights of nature and traditional communities in the region, and the need to protect Brazilian biomes and the planet's future from the interests of multibillion-dollar transnational companies. Additionally, the Tribunal determined that the Federal Government should implement structural changes in decision-making processes and infrastructure planning, strengthen territorial governance, and promote a new vision for Amazonian infrastructure. It reiterated the necessity of Free, Prior, and Informed Consent (FPIC) consultation with Indigenous and traditional peoples for any project that directly or indirectly affects these communities. The sentence highlighted five main arguments for the accusations: violation of the right to free, prior, informed, and good-faith consultation; flawed studies and underestimation of connected socio-environmental impacts and risks; increased land speculation, illegal appropriation of public lands, deforestation, fires, and land conflicts; and the undue favoring of the interests of the transnational companies. Universidade Federal do Oeste do Pará (Ufopa), Kayapó, Munduruku, Tapajós, Quilombas were involved in the tribunal. On the same day as the Court, protesters held a demonstration against Ferrogrão in the Port of Santarém, drawing attention to the impacts of the railway and its relationship with Cargill, one of the international companies interested in implementing the railway, and one of those responsible for its financing.

amazonwatch.org

---

1 The information about this tribunal was translated from this Portuguese version by Dayani Albuquerque: https://terradedireitos.org.br/noticias/noticias/em-tribunal-popular-povos-indigenas-e-comunidades-tradicionais-sentenciam-a-ferrograo-ao-cancelamento/23973

14   Russell Tribunal on Palestine
Brussels | 1950-

The Russell Tribunal on Palestine (RToP) is an international People's Tribunal created for the promotion of peace and justice in the Middle East. The Russell Tribunal has no legal status but acts as a Tribunal of Conscience, of the people faced with injustices and violations of international law. The Russell Tribunal on Palestine (RToP) is composed of eminent people from all states, including Israel, which will be one of the states investigated. The Russell Tribunal on Palestine includes prominent rights activist Angela Davis and ex-Pink Floyd founder Roger Waters. It will identify all the failings in the implementation of this right and, in full view of international public opinion, it will thus examine the various responsibilities that lead to the continued occupation of the Palestinian Territories by Israel and the non-application of the United Nations resolutions, from Resolution 181 of the 29th of November 1947, on the partition of Palestine, to Resolution ES-10/15 of the 20th of July 2004, that acknowledges the Opinion of the International Court of Justice (ICJ) – of the 9th of July 2004 – on the construction of the Wall by Israel in the Occupied Palestinian Territories. Additionally it requests all the UN Member States to acquit themselves of their legal obligations as defined by the ICJ Opinion. The responsibilities of Israel and also of other states, particularly the United States and the Member States of the European Union, the Arab States and the international organizations concerned (United Nations, the European Union, the Arab League) will be scrutinised. The Tribunal also aims, through this approach, to contribute to the mobilization and the involvement of civil society in all the states concerned on the question of Palestine.

15 Second Russell Tribunal on Latin America
Rome and Brussels | 1974-1976

The Russell Tribunal II was a private opinion tribunal, not linked to international organizations, established to analyze and judge the Latin American dictatorships of the 1960s and 1970s. Instituted by ordinary citizens from different parts of the world, they adopted the Universal Declaration of Human Rights of the UN (and similar instruments of the Organization of American States) as a kind of basic law to judge the practices of the continent's dictatorial governments. The name pays homage to the British philosopher Bertrand Russell, who was involved in pacifist actions in the 1950s and 1960s. Some of the most well-known participants were: Gabriel García Márquez, a Colombian writer with a Nobel Prize in Literature laureate, who contributed with his testimony and support to the causes of the tribunal. Another key figure is Pablo Neruda, Chilean poet, also a Nobel Prize in Literature laureate, who participated in and supported the activities of the tribunal. The analysis conducted by the Russell Tribunal on the Brazilian dictatorship was comprehensive, concluding that the regime violated human rights. Therefore, it needed to be defeated and replaced by a democratic regime where human rights would be respected. The main sources used in the research are the proceedings of the Russell Tribunal II, which convened in Rome and Brussels between 1974-1976. Starting with discussions on the Brazilian case, the Tribunal then examined Argentina, Bolivia, and Uruguay, providing a comparative and comprehensive perspective on the American continent under dictatorial governments. These sources form the basis for the title, the spatial-temporal delineation, and the main objective of the Dissertation to be developed: "The contribution of the Russell Tribunal II to the construction of human rights in Brazil (1964 to 1974)." These proceedings were initially published in Italy. In 2014, marking the 50th anniversary of the 1964 civil-military coup, they were translated and published in Brazil in four volumes by professors from the Federal University of Paraíba.

16 Spirit of Mandela International Tribunal
New York | 2021

The Spirit of Mandela coalition (founded in 2018) organized an international tribunal in New York City on October 22-25, 2021 led by Black liberation organizers and former political prisoners, including Jalil Muntaquim, Co-founder of the Jericho movement, under the banner, 'We Still Charge Genocide.' Among their outcome goals was to lay the groundwork for a "'People's Senate' representative of all 50 states, Indigenous Tribes and major religions." As one of the examples of a truly grassroots community based coalition actions, organizers, artists, clergy, political prisoners, and workers of all kinds gathered to hear testimonials and voices of resistance. Organizers of the Spirit of Mandela collective created a verdict document, and curricula to charge the U.S. government, states, and agencies with injurious violations of human rights in five areas: 1. Racist police killings; 2. Hyper Incarceration; 3. Political Incarceration; 4. Environmental Racism; and, 5. Public Health Racism. In addition to initiating the People's Senate, another aim is to establish a Truth & Reconciliation Commission to address the charges as filed, making it possible to create a pathway to peace. The Spirit of Mandela 2021 International Tribunal is one of the most recognized and important examples of People's Tribunals in North America. A podcast called About the People highlights the work of the Tribunal.

spiritofmandela.org

17 Taxpayers Against Genocide
Multiple Locations | 2024-

Taxpayers Against Genocide (TAG) is an organization dedicated to stop the public funding of genocide. Led by a coalition of prominent activists and ordinary citizens from around the country, including Huawida Arraf, a Palestinian-American activist and human rights attorney, TAG uplifts the voices of those who oppose the ongoing genocide of the Palestinian people. When local and regional courts argued that jurisdiction issues prevented them from intervening in the genocidal campaign against the Palestinian people that included well-documented cases of mass killing, dispossession of lands, and the demolition of infrastructure, ordinary taxpayers organized to elevate their complaints to national and international courts. Their argument is that elected officials do not have the right to authorize tax expenditures for war crimes, and in doing so, politicians cause moral and physical harm against the interests of their own people. Moreover, there is no legitimate 'choice' to genocide another people, and so for those who believe this, the only means to delink from genocide is to refuse to support it. TAG raises the crucial questions of accountability, where the exhaustion of their appeals exposes the fact of no representation for this existential concern for justice, thereby laying the grounds for proof of no taxation without representation as proclaimed in the founding documents of the U.S. government. The organization is firmly rooted in a critical, anti-imperialist framework drawing on evidenced harm to expose U.S. politicians who are complicit in genocide by their allocation of public tax dollars to military battalions and regimes accused of war crimes in violation of the Leahy Law as well as the Geneva Convention, and other major bodies of international law.

taxpayersagainstgenocide.org

18   The Hague Group
Multiple Locations | 2025

The Hague group is composed of countries of the Global South who have formed a bloc committed to "coordinated legal and diplomatic measures" in defense of international law and solidarity with the people of Palestine. Chaired by the Republic of Colombia and the Republic of South Africa, The Hague Group launched in January of 2025 and convened in July of 2025 to consolidate their joint statements in an effort to restore international law towards shared principles of "a world where justice prevails over impunity." Supporting universal jurisdiction mandates is the idea that if you are guilty of war crimes anywhere in the world, you can be arrested by any authority who is obligated to follow international law regardless of where the crimes were committed in the first place. In the July 2025 convening, The Hague Group agreed on six items including preventing the provision or transfer of arms, transit, docking, and carrying of arms on vessels and review of public contracts to prevent public institutions and funds from supporting war crimes. The Hague Group meetings heard evidenced review and developed the agreements around supporting accountability measures and universal jurisdiction mandates.

thehaguegroup.org

19   The International Rights of Nature Tribunal
Multiple Locations | 2014-

The tribunal, held concurrently with the COP23, focused on how legal systems contribute to climate change and environmental degradation by legalizing activities harmful to ecological systems. It aimed to demonstrate that effective climate action is impeded by existing laws that prioritize corporate and property rights over environmental and ecological health. The Tribunal was attended by nine judges from seven different countries, with leadership provided by Tom Mato Awanyankapi Goldtooth, a prominent Indigenous climate and environmental justice leader. Participants included 53 individuals from 19 countries, communicating in over seven languages. The witnesses and experts included indigenous peoples from various regions such as Europe, the Amazon, North America, Africa, Russia, Bolivia, Ecuador, and French Guyana. They testified on the violations of the Rights of Nature and shared their personal experiences living near harmful industries like fracking sites and coal mines. The outcomes of the Tribunal highlighted serious and systematic violations of the Universal Declaration of the Rights of Mother Earth (UDRME) across the seven cases examined. These violations often intersected with human rights abuses, some instances were found severe enough to be considered ecocide. These findings pointed out that legal systems frequently fail to provide adequate remedies to prevent ongoing harm, instead granting legal legitimacy to environmentally destructive activities.

rightsofnaturetribunal.org

20   The Special Jurisdiction for Peace / Jurisdicción Especial para la Paz (JEP)
Colombia | 2016-2019

The Special Jurisdiction for Peace or El Tribunal para la Paz (JPE) is the judicial component of the process, which relies on international law to investigate war crimes committed before December 1, 2016. It was created to guarantee and satisfy the rights of victims to justice, provide them with truth, and contribute to their reparation, with the aim of helping to build a stable and lasting peace. Over 200,000 people were killed and 7M people displaced during a 52-year civil war period, half of which under U.S. Plan Colombia that financed the Colombian military and paramilitary forces. The JEP is the fourth element of a transitional justice system that was established as part of the peace agreement to deliver justice to victims of the conflict in Colombia. The other three elements are a Truth Commission, a unit for missing persons, and a reparations program. The tribunal has found that at least 6,402 innocent people were murdered by the country's army and falsely declared combat kills in order to boost statistics at the command of Álvaro Uribe in what is known as the False Positives scandal. That number is nearly three times higher than the figure previously admitted by the attorney general's office. Within a year and a half of its operation, the JEP commenced efforts to mitigate impunity for severe human rights violations and ensure reparations for victims. Over 11,000 individuals have submitted to the JEP, with approximately 820,000 victims identified across seven major cases. The establishment of 19 branches nationwide has facilitated greater interaction with local organizations and authorities, significantly enhancing the JEP's reach and effectiveness.

21   The UC People's Tribunal for Palestine
University of California campuses | 2024-2025

The UC People's Tribunal for Palestine formed as a response to systemic repression against members of the UC system in their efforts to raise consciousness and bring an end to an ongoing genocide of the Palestinian people. The tribunal was organized to denounce the brutal crackdown of the police on unarmed student protestors in Los Angeles, and the continued vilification of students, staff, and faculty. After years of UC leadership failing to condemn genocidal violence in Palestine and yet continuing to actively invest in its devastation, the UC People's Tribunal for Palestine was formed in order to compile evidence, hear testimonies, and speak out to "hold the University of California accountable for complicity in Israel's genocide of the Palestinian people and the ongoing Nakba (catastrophe)." Two sessions were so far held, the first at UCSF and the second at UCSC, in November 2024 and May 2025 respectively. With rallies and teach-ins, a compilation of evidence on a website, and live events with music, art, and ceremony led by major movement leaders and community judges.

ucpeoplestribunal.org

22 Tribunal Unitário Agrário (TUA) Unitary Agrarian Tribunal
Mexico | 1992 - Present

The Unitary Agrarian Tribunal (TUA) is a specialized judicial institution in Mexico, dedicated to resolving agrarian conflicts and protecting the rights of rural communities and agricultural workers. It was created in 1992 with the reform of Article 27 of the Mexican Constitution, which modernized and reorganized the agrarian justice system in the country. The main objective of the TUA is to protect the land ownership and usage rights of ejidatarios, comuneros, and small landowners. This includes resolving disputes over possession, inheritance, land division, and other conflicts related to agricultural land. The procedures in the TUA are designed to be more accessible and less formal than traditional courts, recognizing the need for a justice system that is understandable and usable by rural workers and agrarian communities. This includes the possibility of holding hearings at the location of the disputes, facilitating access to justice. The tribunal is composed of agrarian judges specialized in agrarian law and familiar with the rural reality of Mexico. They are responsible for conducting hearings, evaluating evidence, and issuing judgments. The TUA has resolved numerous land disputes involving ejidatarios (members of agrarian communities), comuneros (members of Indigenous communities), and small landowners. This has helped to reduce conflicts and promote social harmony in rural areas. Also, the tribunal has supported the broader objectives of agrarian reform in Mexico, helping to implement policies aimed at redistributing land and improving rural livelihoods.

tribunalesagrarios.gob.mx

23   The International Tribunal for Democracy in Brasil
Rio de Janeiro | July 19-20, 2016

Initiated by Via Campesina Internacional, Frente Brasil Popular, and Frente Brasil Juristas pela Democracia, the International Tribunal for Democracy in Brazil aimed to broaden the debate and understanding of what these organizations define as a new form of coup d'état (impeachment without a crime of responsibility) in particular in light of the impeachment proceedings charged against Dilma Vana Rousseff. The trial was conducted in three stages. In the first stage, witnesses were heard, and oral arguments were presented by the prosecution and defense. In the second stage, each juror had 30 minutes to cast their vote. In the third stage, the final sentence was pronounced and subsequently forwarded to the Senate and the Supreme Federal Court. Inspired by the Russell Tribunal, which in the 1960s judged the crimes of the United States in the Vietnam War, the Brazilian trial has left an important record in national and international history to recognize the weaponization of lawfare aimed at impeachments of popularly elected governments by singular bodies (Congress) without an election or proper referendum to allow the 'will of the people'. The event took place at Teatro Oi Casa Grande with free admission. The Tribunal for Democracy aimed to clarify the global debate on the impeachment process, making it clear that if the process was not based on a crime of responsibility, it represents a new form of coup d'état, an institutionalized coup by Brazilian senators and congressional representatives.

24   Women's International War Crimes Tribunal on Japan's Military Sexual Slavery
Tokyo | Dec 2000

One of the landmark tribunals addressing the long repressed atrocities of sexual slavery as war crimes of the state, the Women's International War Crimes Tribunal was a major international effort to exact accountability for hundreds of thousands of former 'comfort women' who were forced into sexual slavery by the Japanese Imperial Army during World War II. Conveners were the Violence Against Women in War Network (VAWW-Net Japan), the Korean Council for the Drafted into Military Sexual Slavery in Japan, and the Asian Center for Women's Human Rights (ASCENT). The tribunal broke nearly 55 years of silence for the then-elderly women who experienced this particular form of state-sanctioned brutality, some of whom described recruitment through deception, coercion, kidnapping, and the systematic deployment of shame. Despite being victims of such crimes in the name of the imperial Army even after the Post-WWII San Francisco Peace Treaty (1951), most women endured no relief or reparation for their lifetimes. Indictments for war crimes were received by women from many countries of the Asian Pacific including North and South Korea, Taiwan, Philippines, and East Timor. In the latter case, the European colonial practice of sexual slavery in Dutch-controlled Java was cited. The evidence presented included physical and mental suffering by perpetrators within the ranks of the Japanese state and organized by the highest levels of administration of the Army. Among the accused was Emperor Hiohito. Many of the women lived in extreme poverty and suffered physical and mental illness as a result of the injuries sustained. One of the judges and historians of the Tribunal, Christine Chinkin, stated, "it is a striking example of the developing role of civil society as an international actor. The tribunal built on the earlier examples including the tribunal on Vietnam war crimes instituted by Russell Bertrand in the late 1960s and the Permanent Peoples Tribunal established in Rome.

Contributor Bios

B'eleje' Kan Ed.D. from the School of Education at California State University and is a Bay Area researcher, professor, presenter, writer, Mayan community worker, Mayan resistance member in Guatemala, organizer of the Maya Kaqchikel community in the North of California, coordinator of the Initiative University Maya Mam in California working with Mayan youth populations in the East Bay, and interpreter/practitioner for the Mayan dialectic method Dialogues of Knowledge (DofK). Kan was a fellow with the Democracy + Media Lab (2023-2025).

Angela Marino is an Associate Professor in the Department of Theater, Dance, and Performance Studies at UC Berkeley. Her research focuses on performance and political cultures; festival studies; theater histories, and hemispheric studies. Marino is lead faculty of the Democracy + Media Lab, demoxmedia.org.

Javier Mateos-Campos Ph.D. in the Educational Leadership and Policy Studies program at the University of Texas San Antonio. He is a Mexican immigrant, activist-organizer, and multidisciplinary arts-based researcher whose work focuses on the Chicanx experience in the United States, pedagogies of liberation, and decolonial studies. Javi is also a documentarian, photographer, and visual artist specialized in social movements. Mateos-Campos was a fellow with the Democracy + Media Lab (2023-2025).

Lulu Matute is the Organizing Coordinator for the **School of the Americas Watch** (SOAW), a U.S.-based interfaith organization working to end war and militarization through education, advocacy, and nonviolent resistance. In her role with SOAW, Lulu organizes public events, international delegations, and educational campaigns and projects—bringing together lawmakers, activists, scholars, artists, and grassroots organizers to challenge the impact of U.S. policies fueling militarization, resource extraction, and forced displacement across Latin America. soaw.org

Shaka Shakur is a committed New Afrikan revolutionary and a political prisoner who has been incarcerated since 2002 on trumped up charges. He is a dedicated husband, father, grandfather, and community member from Gary, Indiana. Ever since he became politically aware as a young man, Shaka has been a steadfast organizer for the collective liberation of Afrikan people and all people everywhere. Shaka's incisive writing makes clear the purpose and techniques of carceral institutions, as well as the imperative for liberation both inside and outside of the prison. He is featured in radio and podcast interviews from Black Agenda Report to Re-Build (the newspaper of the New Afrikan Independence movement) and the Bayview Press to name a few. shakashakur.org

Judith Talaugon is a Chumash and Filipina Land Protector from the Santa Ynez Band of Chumash Indians. She is the daughter of farmworkers and immigrant leaders. Growing up among Mexican and Filipina communities in California, she has been a long-time activist in numerous struggles, ranging from human rights to housing, land rights, and the fight against white supremacy. She participated in the shutting down of the quincentennial celebration of the myth of discovery by Christopher Columbus and the genocidal practices against Indigenous communities in the Western Hemisphere. Talaugon is an Organizer for CICEP: California Indians for Cultural and Environmental Protection and led Genocide, Colonialism, and Resistance workshops to train people to confront white supremacy in the late 1990s. She has been active throughout the state of California and in many parts of the world on projects focusing on housing rights, land back struggles, and the protection of water and land defenders. She consistently uplifts BIPOC women in the movement. Her work is based on clear principles aimed at creating a culture of resistance, standing in solidarity with activists from the entire hemisphere and world, and building up women-led Indigenous landback movements alongside and in solidarity with Black, AAPI, and Latinx communities. Talaugon was a fellow with the Democracy + Media Lab (2023-2025).

Editors and authors contributing chapters in this book extend their appreciation to all the participants of the Tribunal Project and the D+M Lab including invited scholars, writers, and artists to Tribunal events: Jorge García, Tiokasin Ghosthorse, John Lindsay Poland, Hector Muñoz-Guzmán, Melissa Nelson, Alberto Saldomando, and Lilia Soto. We are especially grateful to Eleni Berg, Biel Delgado, Katherine García, Alexander Quiroz, and Dr. Abraham Ramírez for their contributions at different stages of this book planning.

Featured writers of the Part Two art exhibit compendium are:
Sarine Danielle Baronian, Delmi Belloso, Alexander Cole, Brandon Cruz, Muhammad Delgado, Keira Duong Lam, Theodore Dupont, Jonas Kramer, Alexander Marsh, Ci Mingshu, Juna Park, Abby Román, and Jingyi Zhou.

www.ingramcontent.com/pod-product-compliance
Lightning Source LLC
Chambersburg PA
CBHW021151130626
46554CB00005B/1755